BAROQUE ART

Author: Klaus H. Carl & Victoria Charles

Layout:
Baseline Co. Ltd,
District 10, Ho Chi Minh City
Vietnam

ISBN: 978-1-68325-915-2

Printed in

Klaus H. Carl & Victoria Charles

BAROQUE ART

Drama, grandeur, and the power
of light and shadow

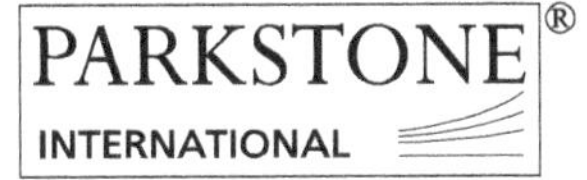

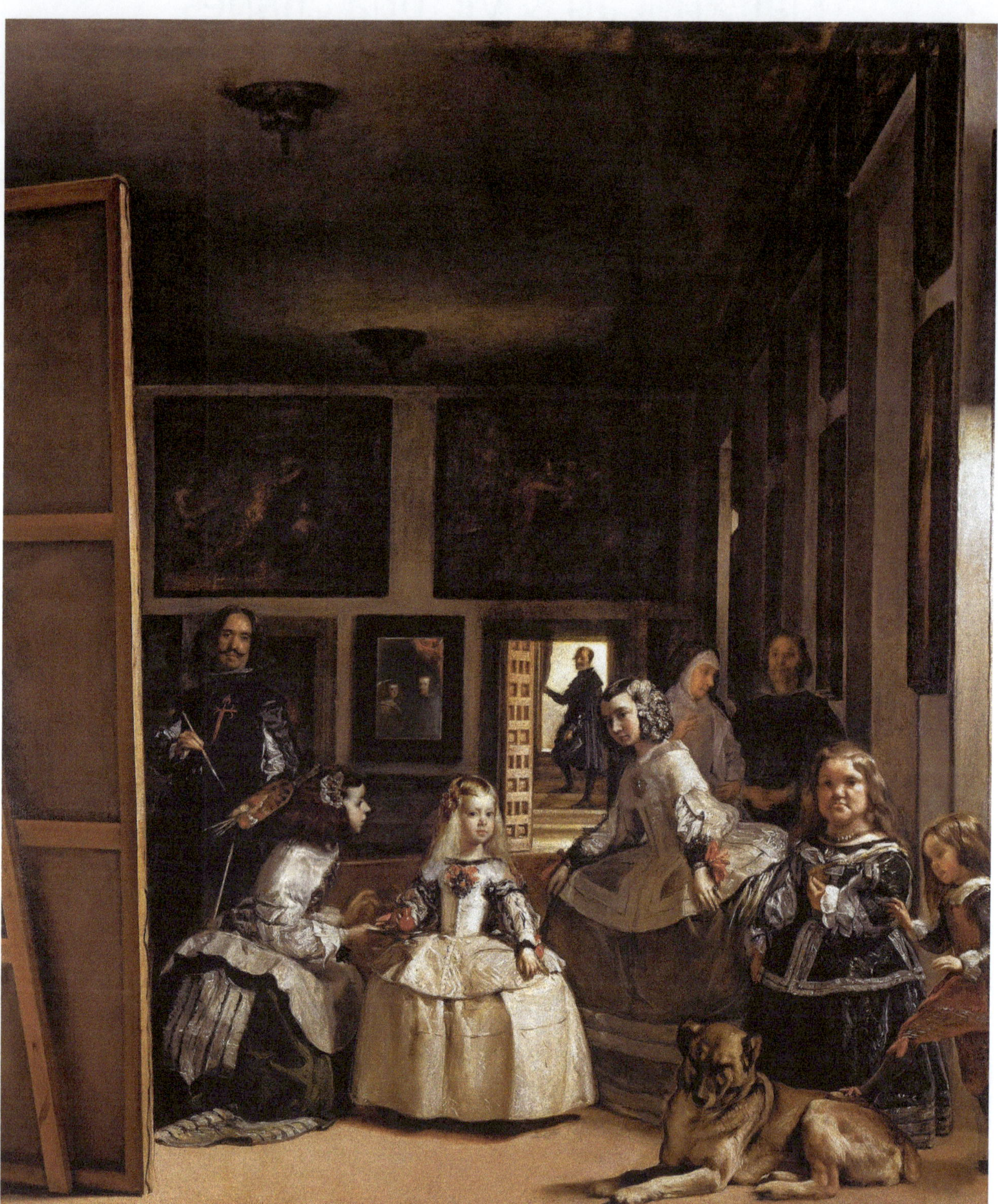

CONTENTS

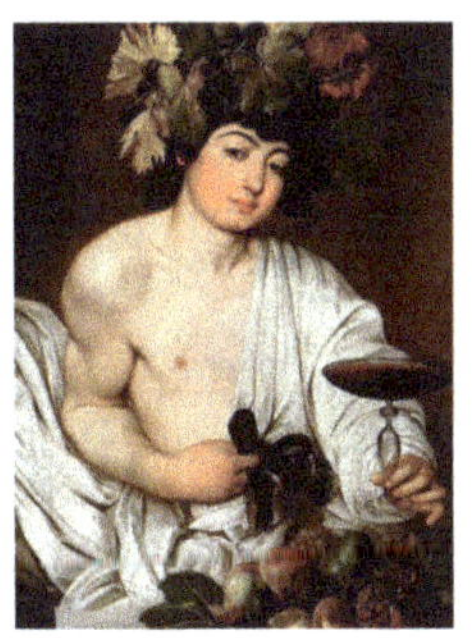
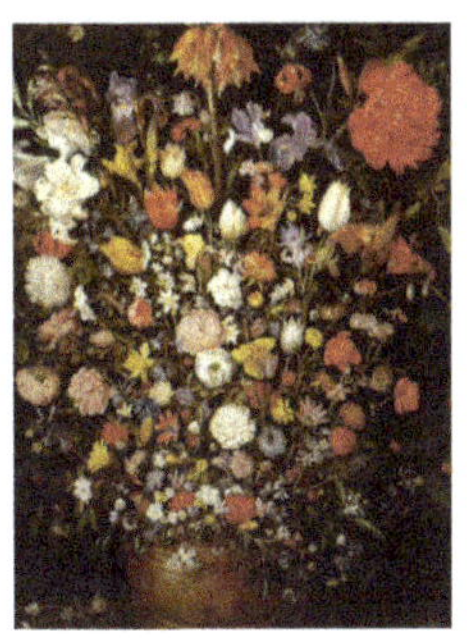
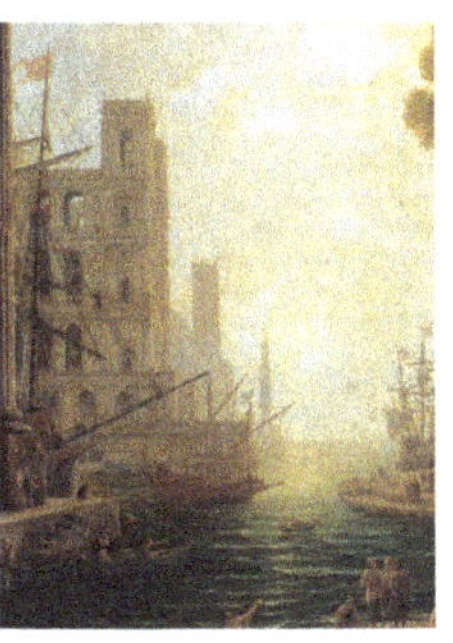
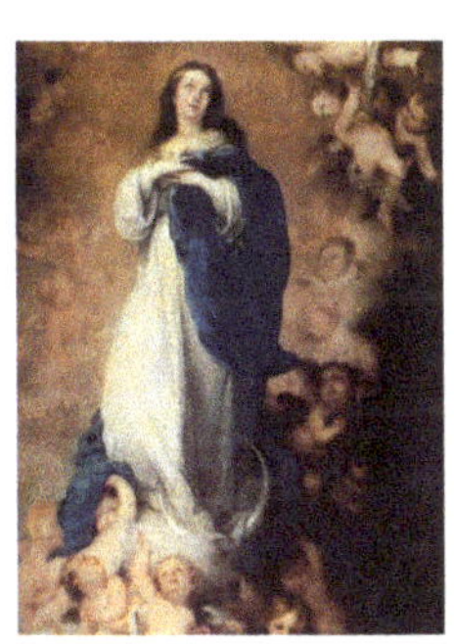
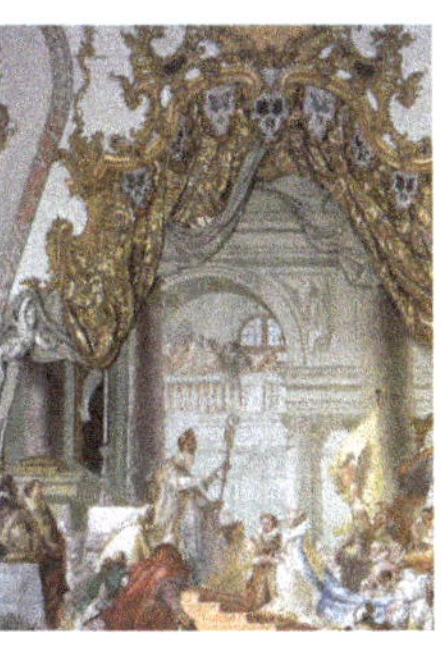

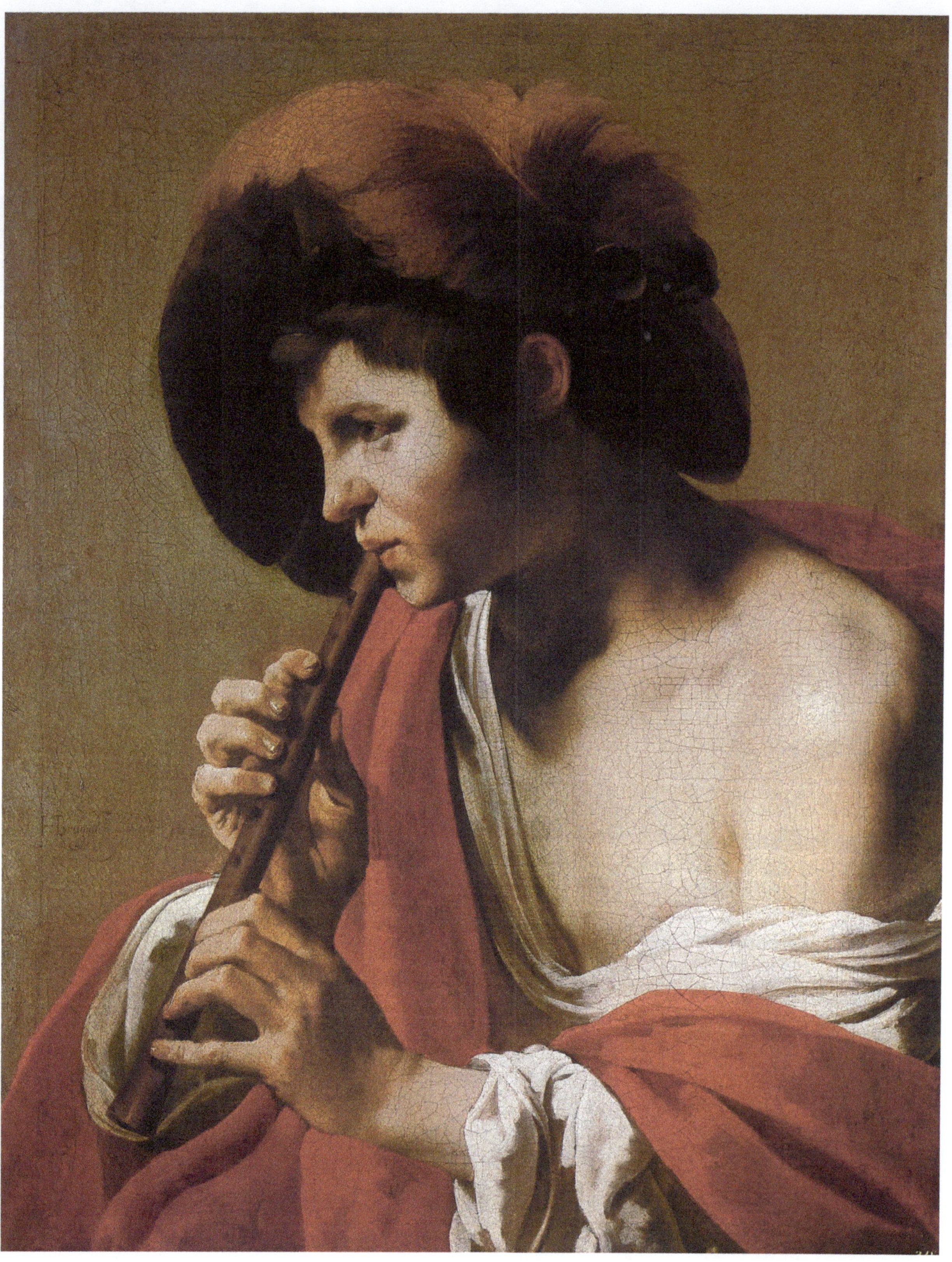

FOREWORD

Baroque art (derived from the Portuguese word 'Barrocco' meaning rough or imperfect pearl) originated in Italy and a few other countries as an imperceptible passage from the late Renaissance which ended about 1600. It roughly coincides with the 17th century.

The word Baroque was for a time confined to the craft of the jeweller. It indicates the most extravagant fashions of design that were common in the first half of the 18th century, chiefly in Italy and France, in which everything is fantastic, grotesque, florid or incongruous – irregular shapes, meaningless forms, an utter lack of restraint and simplicity. The word suggests much the same order of ideas as Rococo.

It was occasionally seen as a variation and brutalization of the Renaissance style and sometimes conversely as a higher form of its development, and remained dominant until approximately the middle of the eighteenth century. Conventionally, the Baroque style is not emphasized in the global history of art, because the time period when it flourished – between 1550 and 1750 – is correctly viewed as an enclosed time period in which various directions of style were expressed. The work that distinguishes the Baroque period is stylistically complex and even contradictory.

Baroque art is applicable to sculpture architecture, furniture and literature. The seventeenth century also brought Baroque innovations in music.

▲ **Diego Velázquez,**
Las Meninas, 1656-1657.
Oil on canvas, 318 x 276 cm.
Museo Nacional del Prado, Madrid.

◀ **Hendrick Ter Brugghen,**
Flute Player, 1621.
Oil on canvas, 71.3 x 55.8 cm.
Staatliche Museum, Gemäldegalerie Alte Meister, Kassel.

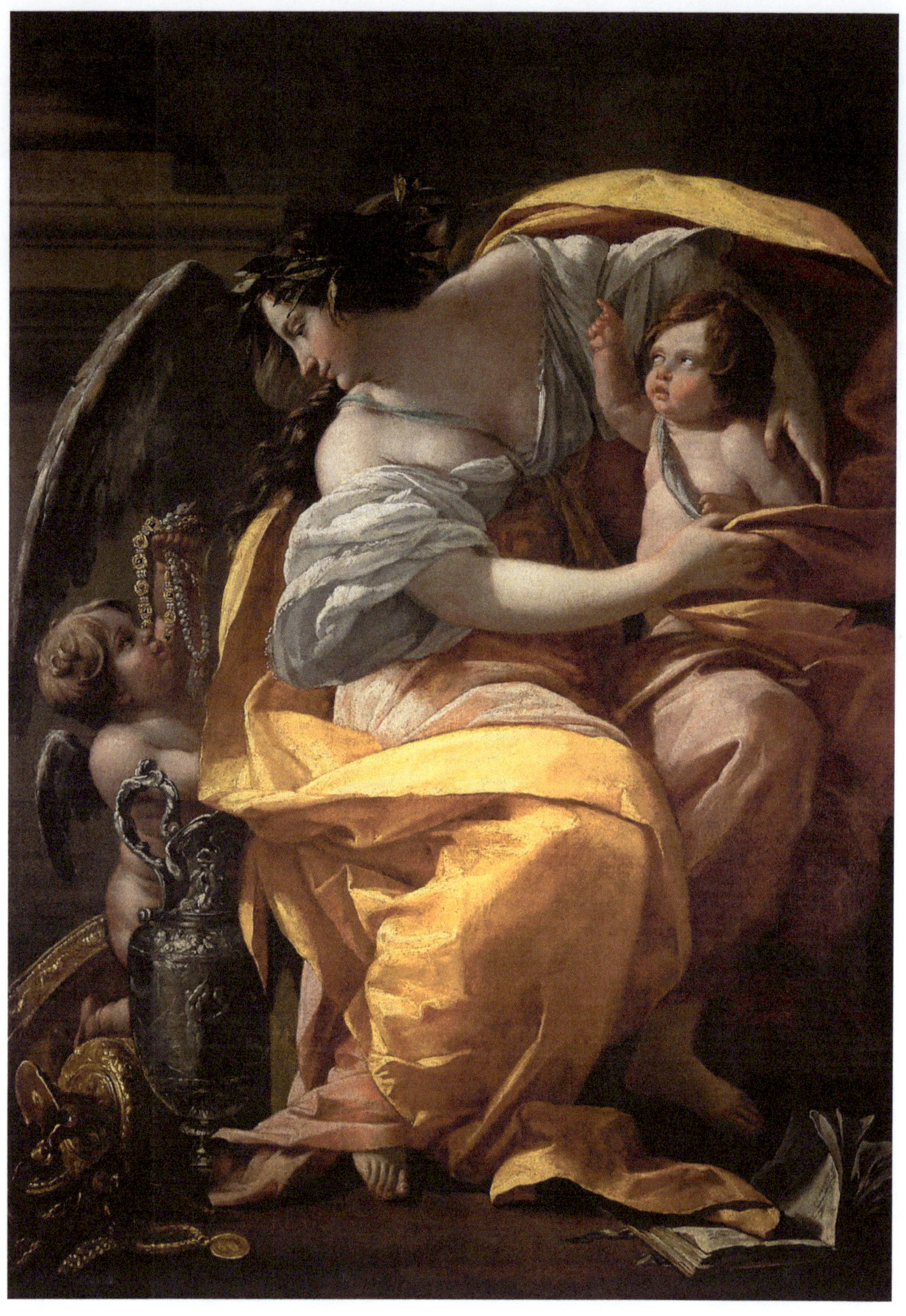

BAROQUE ART

While Italian Renaissance artists created highly organised spatial settings and idealised figures, northern Europeans focused on everyday reality and on the variety of life. Few painters have equalled the Netherlandish painter Jan Van Eyck, for example, in his close observation of surfaces, and captured more clearly and poetically the glint of light on a pearl, the deep, resonant colours of a red cloth, or the glinting reflections that appear in glass and on metal.

Spanning both north and south Europe during the Renaissance was Albrecht Dürer of Nuremburg. Durer followed the Italian practice of canonical measure of the human body and perspective, though he retained the emotional expressionism and sharpness of line that was widespread in German art. Though he shared the optimism of Italians, many other northern painters were pessimistic about the human condition. Giovanni Pico della Mirandola's essay on the Dignity of Man presaged Michelangelo's belief in the perfectibility and essential beauty of the human body and soul, but Erasmus's Praise of Folly and Sebastian Brant's satirical poem Ship of Fools belonged to the same northern European cultural milieu that produced the fantastic visions of Hieronymus Bosch's Garden of Earthly Delights triptych and Pieter Bruegel's raucous peasant scenes. There was hope for humankind in paradise, but little consolation on earth for beings consumed by their passions and caught in an endless cycle of desire and fruitless yearning. Northern humanists, like their Italian counterparts, called for the classical virtues of moderation, restraint and harmony – the pictures of Bruegel represented the very vices against which they warned. Unlike some of the contemporary Romanists, who had travelled from the Netherlands to Italy and been inspired by Michelangelo and other artists of the time, Bruegel travelled to Rome around 1550 but remained largely untouched by its art. Instead he turned to local inspiration and staged his scenes amidst humble settings, earning him the undeserved nickname 'Peasant Bruegel'. Brueghel was a herald of the realism and bluntness of the northern European Baroque.

◀ **Simon Vouet**, *Wealth*, 1627.
Oil on canvas, 107 x 142 cm.
Musée du Louvre, Paris.

The great intellectual revolt set in motion by theologians Martin Luther and John Calvin in the sixteenth century provoked the Catholic Church to respond to the challenge of the Protestants. Various church councils called for reform of the Roman Catholic Church, and participants at the Council of Trent declared that religious art should be simple and accessible to a broad public. A number of Italian painters, however, known as Mannerists, had begun developing a form of art that was complex in subject matter and style. Painters eventually responded to ecclesiastical needs as well as to the stylisations of Mannerism. We call this new era the age of the Baroque, which was ushered in initially by Caravaggio. He painted mainly religious subject matter, but in the most realistic and dramatic manner possible, and gained a following among ordinary people as well as among connoisseurs and even Church officials. Caravaggism swept across Italy and then the rest of Europe, as a host of painters came to adopt his chiaroscuro and suppression of vivid colouring; his earthy tones and powerful figures struck a chord with viewers across the continent who had tired of some of the artificialities of sixteenth-century art.

In addition to the Caravaggism of the early Baroque, another form of painting later called the High Baroque – the most dramatic, dynamic and painterly style yet seen – also developed, built on the foundations laid by the sixteenth-century Venetians. Peter Paul Rubens, an admirer of Titian, painted huge canvases with fleshy figures, rich landscapes, broken brushwork and flickering light and dark tones. His pictorial experiments were the starting point for the art of other northern European artists such as Anthony Van Dyck; the latter had a large following among the European elite for his noble portrait manner. Rubens brought back the world of antiquity, painting ancient gods and goddesses, but his style was anything but classical. He found a ready market for his works among European aristocrats who liked his exuberance, and among Catholic patrons of art who found in his flamboyant sacred scenes a weapon for Counter-Reformation ideology. In Rome, Bernini was Ruben's counterpart in sculpture, providing the Catholic Church with two powerful champions for the power and majesty of the Church and Papacy. Italian Baroque painters unleashed a torrent of holy figures on the ceilings of churches in Rome and other cities, with the skies opening up to reveal Heaven itself and God's personal acceptance of the martyrs and mystics of Catholic sainthood. The Spanish painters Velasquez, Murillo and Zurburán also took up the style, using quieter movement and brushwork, but sharing with the Italians a mystical sense of light and Catholic iconography.

How different from all this were the paintings of seventeenth-century Holland! Having effectively freed themselves from Habsburg Spain by the 1580s, the Dutch practised a tolerant form of Calvinism, which eschewed religious iconography.

Michelangelo Merisi da Caravaggio, ▶
The Martyrdom of St. Matthew, 1599-1600,
Oil on canvas, 323 x 343 cm.
San Luigi dei Francesi, Rome.

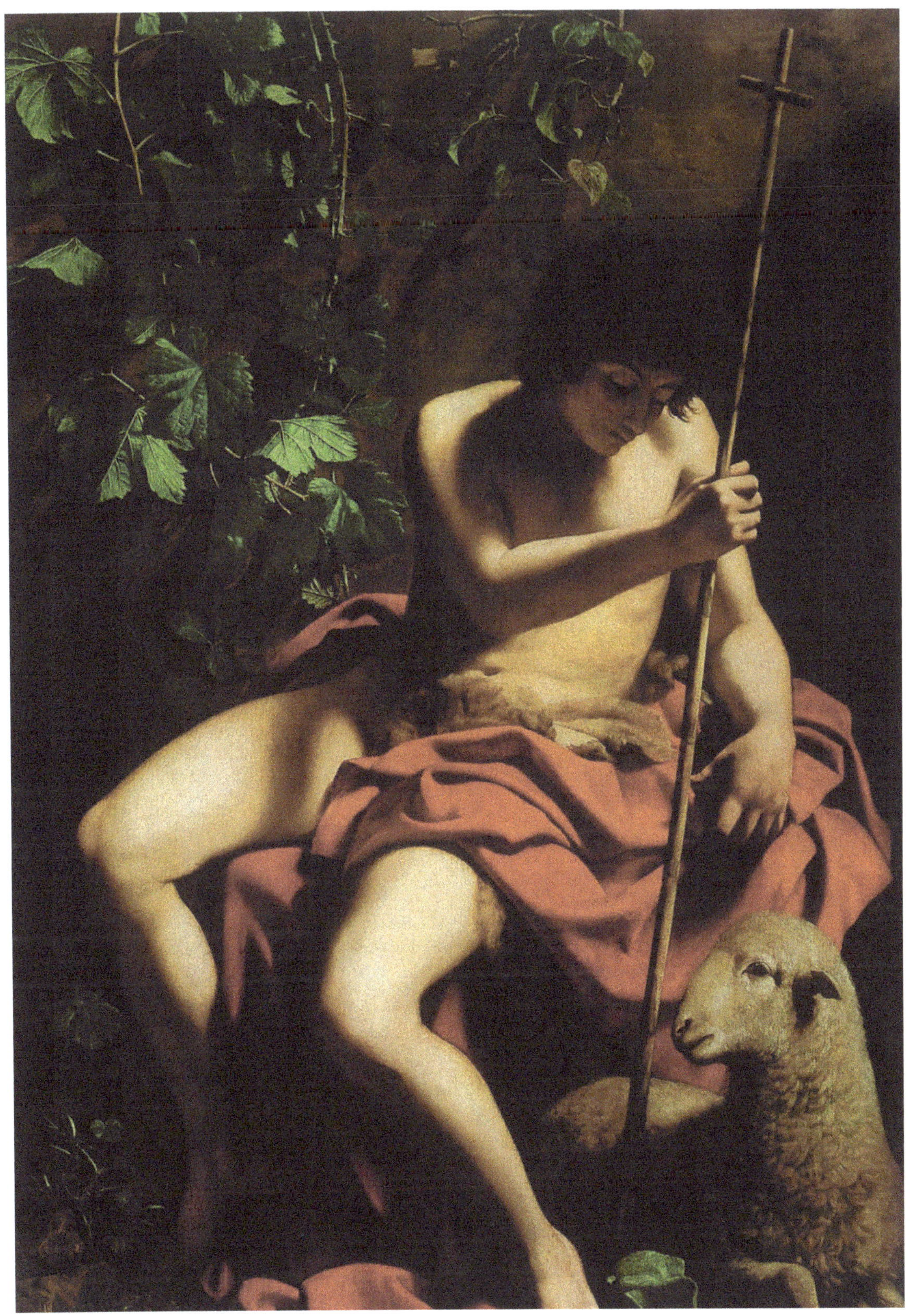

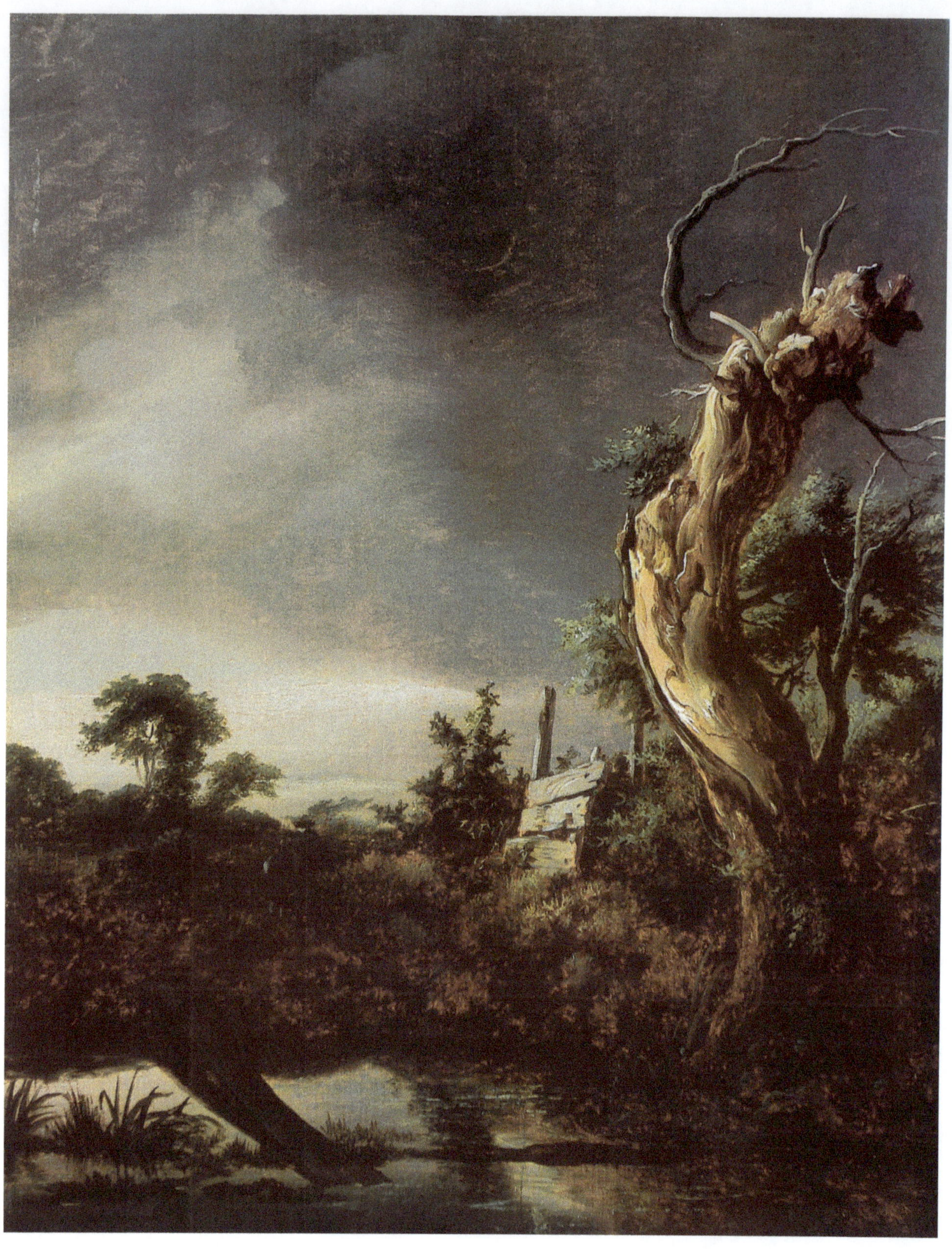

A growing middle class and increasingly wealthy upper class acted as patrons for the delightful variety of secular paintings produced by a host of skilled painters, with individual artists specialising in moonlit landscapes, skating and tavern scenes, still-lifes, domestic interiors, ships at sea and a great variety of other subjects. From this large school of artists several individual painters stand out. Jacob van Ruisdael is the closest we have to a High Baroque landscape painter in Holland – his dark and sometimes stormy landscapes evoke the drama and movement widespread in European art of the time. Like Ruisdael, Frans Hals' painting, with its flashy, quick strokes of the brush and exaggerated colouring of skin and garments, approaches a pan-European sensibility of the High Baroque. In contrast, Jan Steen typified the realism and local character of most Dutch art of the Golden Age, and added a moral slant through the depiction of households in disarray and misbehaving peasants. Finally, the paintings of Rembrandt van Rijn stand alone, even amongst the Dutch. Raised as a Calvinist, Rembrandt shared some beliefs with the Mennonites, and was happy to depart from Calvinist strictures against representing biblical scenes. His later paintings, with their quiet introspection, make the perfect Protestant counterpart to the showy, dynamic Roman Catholic paintings of Rubens. From his early, tighter technique influenced by Dutch 'fine painters', Rembrandt developed a broad, shadowy manner derived from Caravaggio, but expressed with much greater pictorial complexity. This style later fell out of favour among the Dutch, but Rembrandt remained true to it, leaving a legacy that would be admired by nineteenth-century Romantic painters and modernists with a taste for painterly abstraction. Rembrandt was also distinctive for the universality of his art, which was steeped in knowledge of other styles and literary sources. Although he never travelled to Italy, he absorbed many of the tenets of Italian painting, and included in his works elements inspired by artists such as the late Gothic artist Antonio Pisanello and the Renaissance masters Mantegna, Raphael and Dürer. His style evolved constantly, and he had the broadest artistic mind and deepest understanding of the human condition of any painter of his age.

Clearly, just as there were many 'Renaissances' in art, there were many forms of the Baroque, and the High Baroque was challenged by the Classical Baroque, which had its philosophical roots in ancient thought and its stylistic basis in the paintings of Raphael and other High Renaissance classicists. Annibale Carracci had embraced a classical approach, and painters like Andrea Sacchi challenged the supremacy in Rome of High Baroque painters like Pietro da Cortona. However, the quintessential classicist of the seventeenth century was the Frenchman Nicolas Poussin, who developed a style perfectly suited to the growing ranks of philosophical Stoics in France, Italy and elsewhere. His solid, idealised figures, endowed with broad physical

◄ **Jacob van Ruisdael**,
Landscape during a Storm, 1649.
Oil on canvas, 25.5 x 21.5 cm.
Musée Fabre, Montpellier.

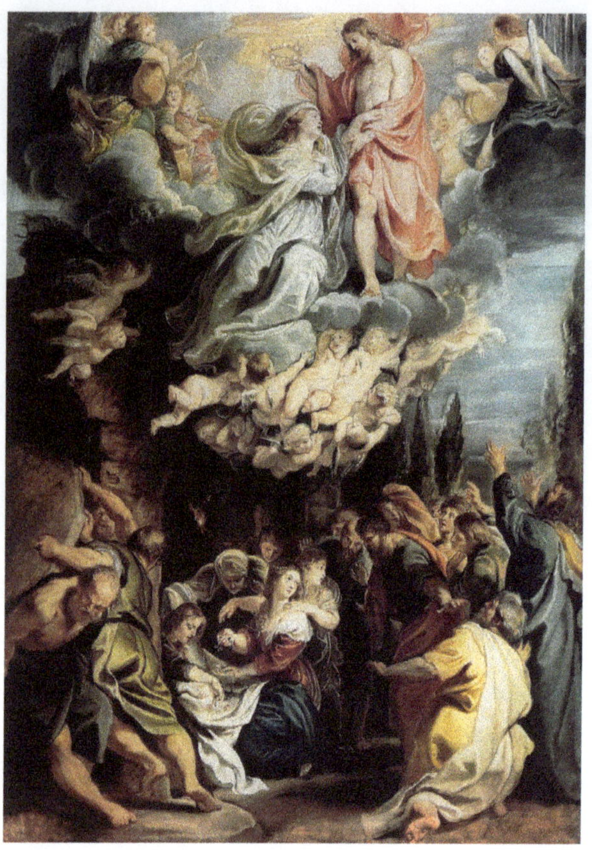

away, waters ripple subtly and hazy views of infinity appear in the distance. Yet both painters conveyed a sense of moderation and balance, and appealed to similar kinds of patrons. All these painters of the seventeenth century, whether or not classical in temperament, participated in the explosion of subject matter of the time; not since antiquity had art-making seen such diversity of iconography of both sacred and profane subjects. With the exploration of new continents, contact with new and different peoples across the globe, and novel views offered by telescopes and microscopes, the world seemed to be an evolving and fractured place and the diversity of artistic styles and pictorial subject matter reflected this dynamism.

Louis XIV (d. 1715), the self-designated Sun King who modelled himself after Apollo and Alexander the Great, favoured the classical mode of Poussin and of painters such as his court artist Charles Le Brun, who, in turn, glorified the king with a number of murky paintings celebrating his reign. There arose at the end of the seventeenth and beginning of the eighteenth century a debate over style, in which painters allied themselves with one of two camps – the Poussinists and the Rubensists. The former favoured classicism, linearity and moderation, while the latter group declared the innate primacy of free colouring, energetic movement and compositional dynamism. When Louis XIV died, the field in France was open, and the Rubensists took the lead, bringing forth a style we call Rococo, which – roughly translated – means 'pebble work Baroque', a decorative version of painterly Baroque.

movements and firm moral purpose, acted out a range of narratives, both sacred and secular. Another Frenchman developed a different form of classicism: the Epicurean paintings of Claude Lorrain at first seem to differ sharply from those of Poussin: in Claude's pictures edges melt

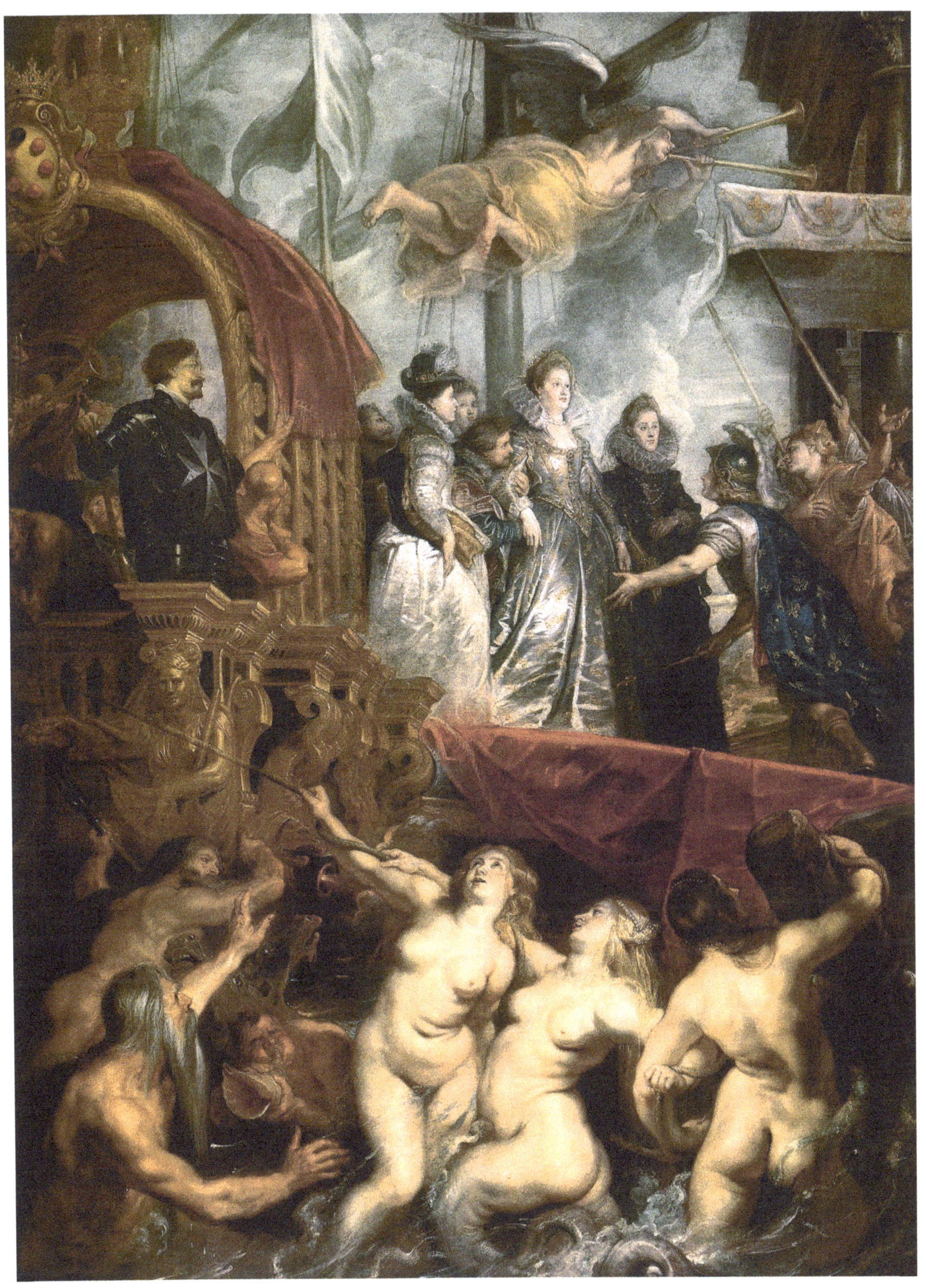

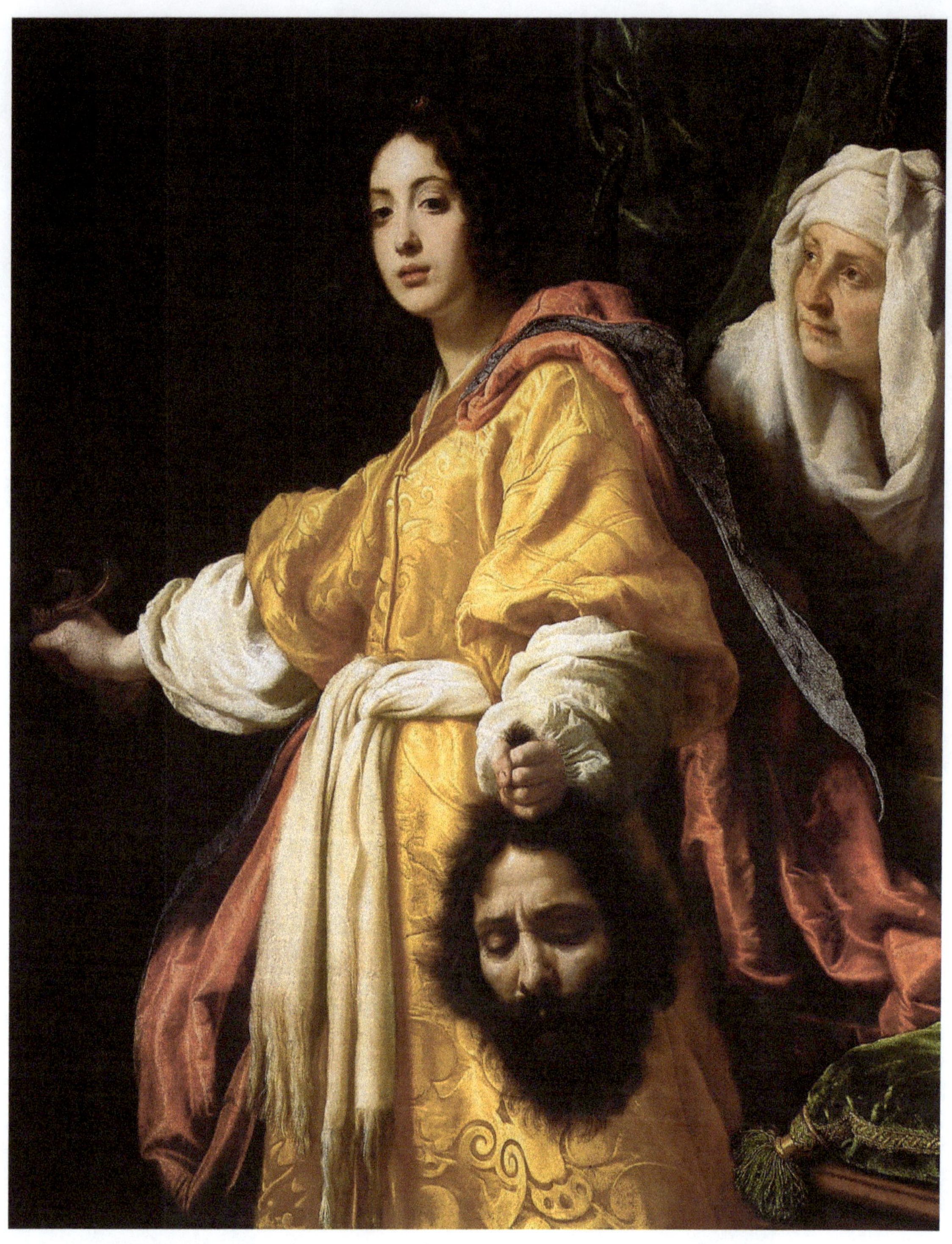

▲**Cristofano Allori,**
Judith with the Head of Holofernes, c. 1613.
Oil on canvas, 120.4 x 100.3 cm. Palazzo Pitti, Florence.

THE ARTISTS

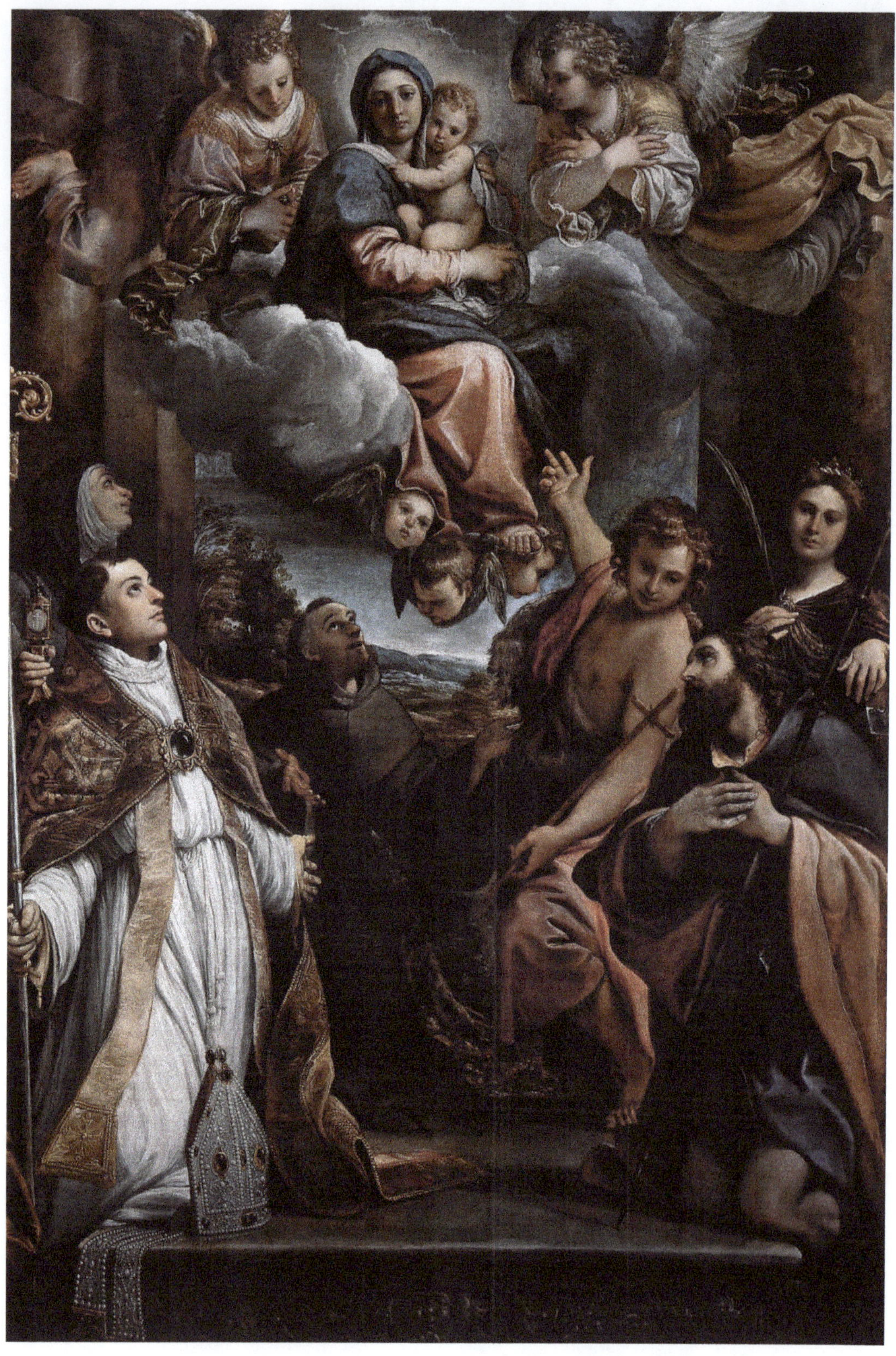

ITALY

The Carraccis

(Bologna 1560 – Rome 1609)

This direction of Italian art, known as Eclecticism, originated in Bologna. The painter Ludovico Carracci, with his cousins Agostino, who became famous for his erotic etchings, and Annibale, known mostly for his frescos, had founded an influential school of painters at the end of the sixteenth century, an academy that promoted all fields of the painting and drawing trades. The pupils were taught all that was worth copying and were kept away from Mannerism.

The greatest combined work of the Carraccis was the decoration of the Large Gallery of the Roman Palazzo Farnese, and they received help from the best pupils of the academy: Giovanni Lanfranco, Guido Reni and Domenico Zampieri, named Domenichino. They were not quite successful but they did create a unified decoration with a great deal of painting

mastery that can be compared with the masterworks of Raphael and Michelangelo. The presentation of the volutes, medallions with small mythological pictures between the nudes, molding supports and winged putti (cherubim) clearly show the influence of Michelangelo, and the main pictures in the mirror of the ceiling show the influence of Raphael. The most beautiful pictures are Agostino's Abduction of Galatea by Polyphemus and Annibale Carracci's Triumph of Bacchus and Ariadne. The finest of his altarpieces is that of Christ who appears to Peter with the Cross on his shoulder as Peter is fleeing from Rome in fear of a martyr's death in the Campagna.

Domenichino, who was mainly active in Rome, was of a somewhat simpler nature, and died after a life that was made miserable mainly by the jealousy of the Neapolitans. Even though he painted very beautiful pictures such as the Hunt of Diana in the Villa Borghese, his main focus was still on religious painting. He was first among the Italians in the seventeenth century to emphasize the moment of religious ecstasy. His main work in this direction is the Communion of Saint Hieronymus in the Vatican Gallery.

◄ **Annibale Carracci,**
Madonna in Glory with Child, St. *Louis, St. John the Baptist,*
St. Alexius, St. Catherine, St. Francis and St. Clare, c. 1587-1588.
Oil on canvas, 278 x 173 cm.
Pinacoteca Nazionale di Bologna, Bologna.

Michelangelo Amerighi Caravaggio (or Merigi)

(1475 Caprese – 1564 Rome)

Caravaggio was born in the village of Caravaggio, in Lombardy, from which he received his name. He was originally a mason's labourer, but his powerful genius directed him to painting, at which he worked with immitigable energy and amazing force. He despised every sort of idealism whether noble or emasculate, became the head of the Naturalisti (unmodified imitators of ordinary nature) in painting, and adopted a style of potent contrasts of light and shadow, laid on with a sort of fury, indicative of that fierce temper which led the artist to commit a homicide in a gambling quarrel at Rome.

To avoid the consequences of his crime he fled to Naples and to Malta, where he was imprisoned for another attempt to avenge a quarrel. Escaping to Sicily, he was attacked by a party sent in pursuit of him, and severely wounded. Being pardoned, he set out for Rome, but having been arrested by mistake before his arrival, and afterwards released, and left to shift for himself in excessive heat, and still suffering from wounds and hardships, he died of fever on the beach of Pontecole in 1609. His best paintings are the Entombment of Christ, St. Sebastian, a magnificent whole-length portrait of a grand-master of the Knights of Malta, Alof de Vignacourt, and his page, and the Borghese Supper at Emmaus.

Michelangelo Merisi da Caravaggio, ▶
Bacchus, c. 1596,
Oil on canvas, 95 x 85 cm.
Galleria degli Uffizi, Florence.

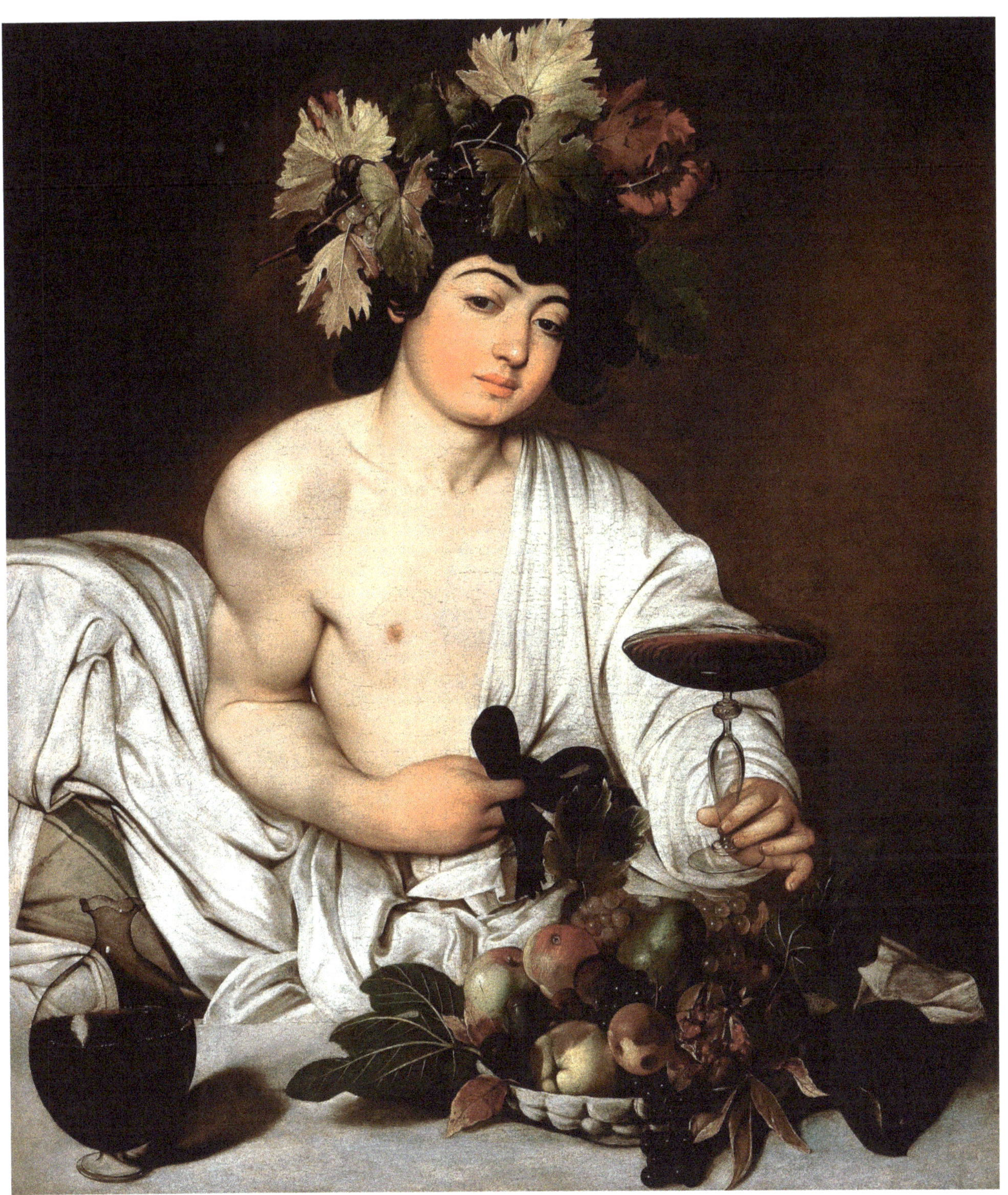

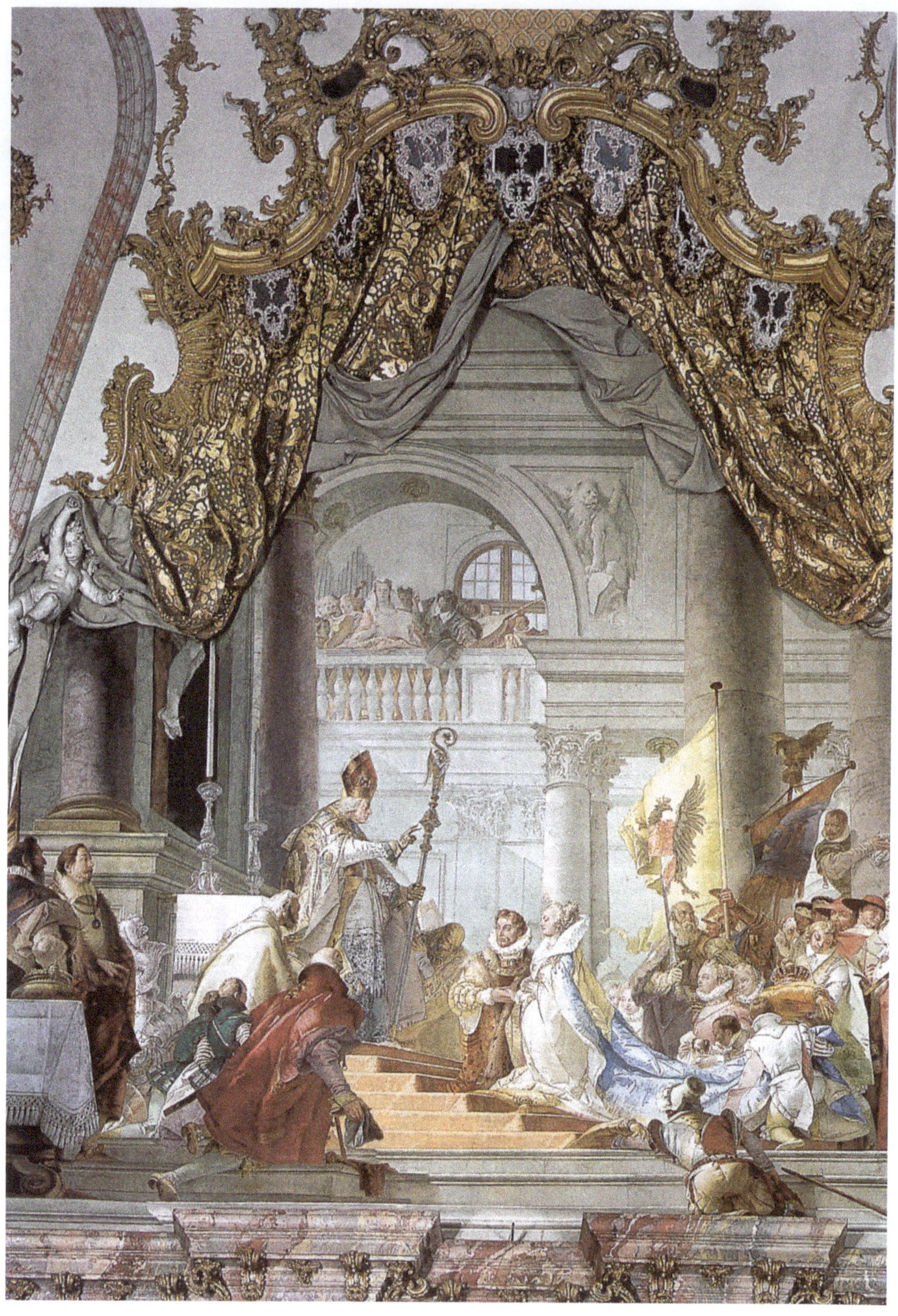

Giovanni Battista Tiepolo

(1696 Venice – 1770 Madrid)

Giovanni Battista (Giambattista) Tiepolo was the last of the great Venetian decorators and the purest master of the Italian Rococo. He was a prodigy, a pupil of Gregorio Lazzarini, but already by age twenty-one he was established as a painter in Venice. He was an Italian artist of large-scale frescos, such as for the Residence in Würzburg and the Palacio Real in Madrid, both of which he did with his sons, Giovanni Domenico and Lorenzo, when he was in his fifties. In 1755, after his return from Würzburg, he was elected the first President of the Venetian Academy, before leaving for Spain where he died.

◀ **Giovanni Battista Tiepolo**, 1696-1770, Rococo, Italian, *The Ceiling of the Kaisersaal: The Marriage of The Emperor Frederick Barbarosa and Beatrice of Burgundy*, 1750-1753. Fresco, 400 x 500 cm. Residence of the prince-bishop of Würzburg, Kaisersaal, Würzburg Residenz.

▼ **Giovanni Battista Tiepolo**, 1696-1770, Rococo, Italian, *The Finding of Moses*, 1730. Oil on canvas, 202 x 342 cm. National Gallery of Scotland, Edinburgh.

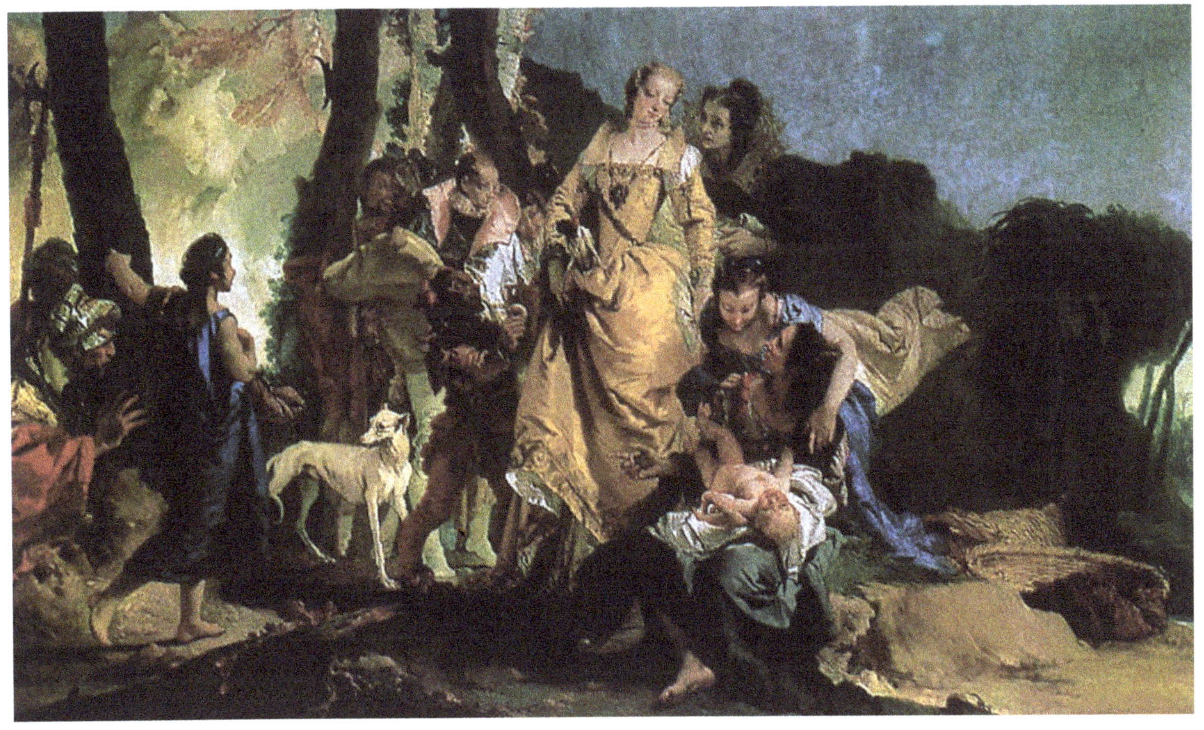

Canaletto (Giovanni Antonio Canal)

(1697 – 1768 Venice)

Canaletto began his career as a theatrical scene painter, like his father, in the Baroque tradition. Influenced by Giovanni Panini, he is specialised in vedute (views) of Venice, his birth place. Strong contrast between light and shadow is typical of this artist. Furthermore, if some of those views are purely topographical, others include festivals or ceremonial subjects.

He also published, thanks to John Smith, his agent, a series of etchings of Cappricci. His main purchasers were British aristocracy because his views reminded them of their Grand Tour. In his paintings geometrical perspective and colours are structuring. Canaletto spent ten years in England. John Smith sold Canaletto's works to George III, creating the major part of the Royal Canaletto Collection. His greatest works influenced landscape painting in the nineteenth century.

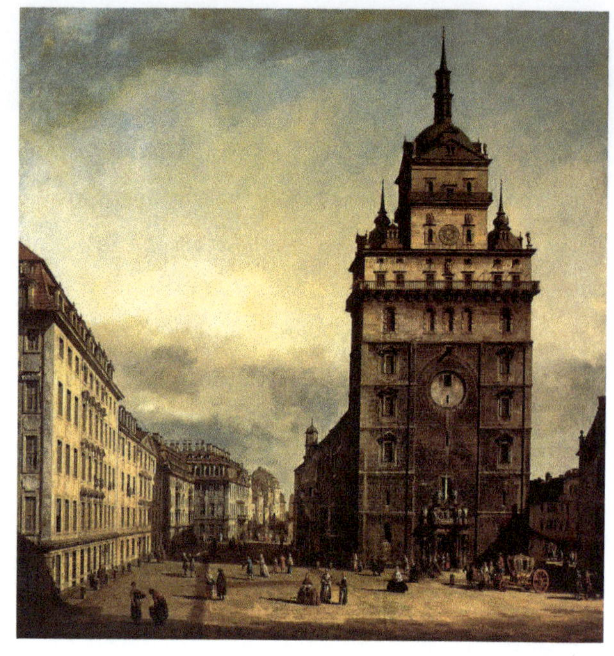

Canaletto (Giovanni Antonio Canal), ▲
1697-1768, Italian, Dresden,
View from the Right Bank of the Elbe, 1747.
Oil on canvas, 133 x 237 cm.
Gemäldegalerie Alte Meister, Dresden.

Canaletto (Giovanni Antonio Canal), 1697-1768, ▶
Rococo, Italian, *The Bucintoro at the Molo on Ascension Day,* 1732.
Oil on canvas, 182 x 259 cm.
Aldo Crespi Collection, Milan.

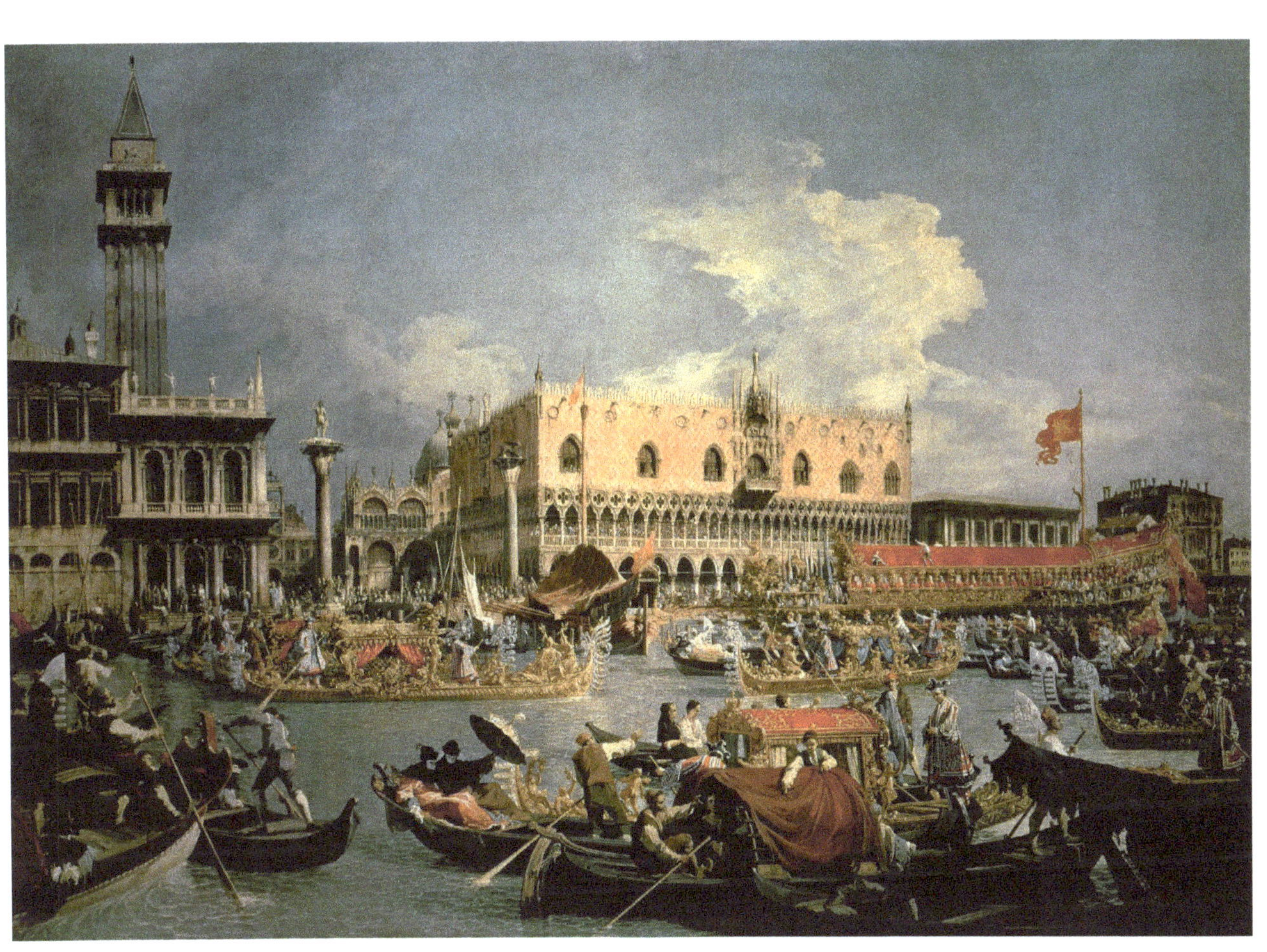

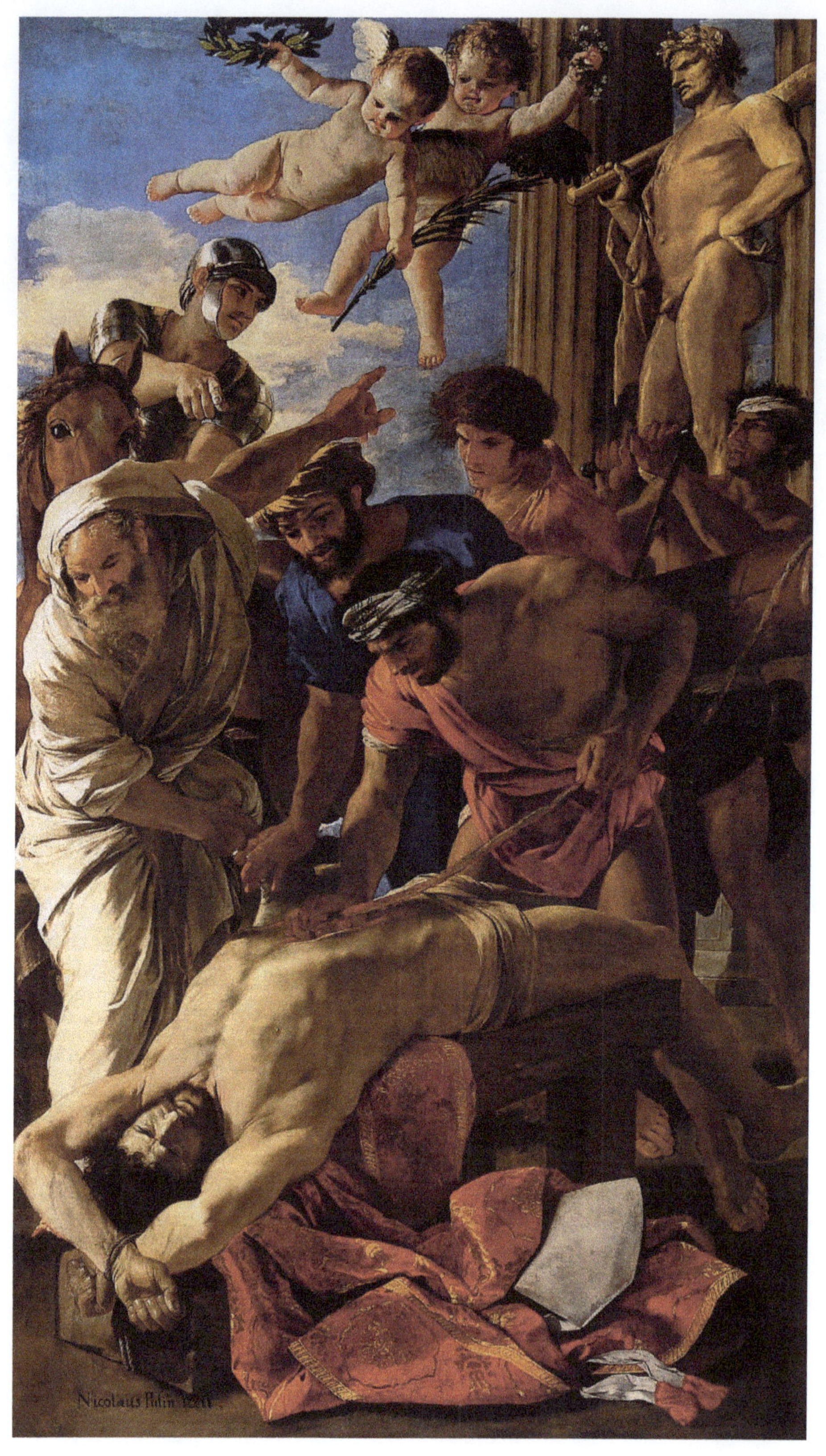

FRANCE

Nicolas Poussin

(1594 Villiers – 1665 Rome)

Although Nicolas Poussin was only four years younger than Vouet, his influence made itself felt in France much later. He was not precocious like Vouet, but may be numbered amongst those great men who have need of reflection and meditation, whose inspiration comes only with maturity. None of his early works has been preserved. His career begins, historically speaking, in 1624 with his arrival in Rome at the age of thirty. He came to Italy in quest of Raphael, whose genius he had discerned from the engravings of Marc-Antoine while still in Paris.

However, Titian was a profound surprise to him, and from that time onwards his constant preoccupation was to reconcile the spirit of these two great men. At times he seemed to prefer a method hovering between these magnetic poles, and vacillated between the linear element derived from Raphael and the warm and coloured atmosphere which he admired in Titian. This clear-sighted and impassioned study which Poussin devoted to Raphael and Titian appears perfectly natural today, but this was not so in 1624, when foreign artists in Rome had no eyes except for the Academic art derived from the Bolognese or from the brutal naturalism of the disciples of Caravaggio. Poussin equally detested both, and with his robust, philosophical frankness, condemned both unsparingly. The finest aspect of Poussin's genius is to have put into his masterpieces more thought than it was ever given to any other painter to express, and to have found for that poetic and philosophical thought an original and plastic interpretation. Poussin is one of the greatest landscape painters. His sketches are comparable only to those of Lorrain, and are perhaps yet finer. Poussin is inferior to Titian in richness of colour as well as fullness and purity of form; but his poet philosopher's genius added a lofty spirituality and an indefinable touch of the heroic to the symphony of man and nature. Poussin, who from the age of thirty spent most of his life in Rome, remains the most French of the great painters, and always kept in view that wise and noble balance between reason and feeling.

◄ **Nicolas Poussin,**
The Martyrdom of St. Erasmus, 1628-1629.
Oil on canvas, 320 x 186 cm.
Pinacoteca, Vatican.

Claude Lorrain (Claude Gellée)

(1604 Chamagne – 1682 Rome)

Claude Gellée, called Claude Lorrain was neither a great man nor a lofty spirit like Poussin. His genius cannot, however, be denied and he was, like Poussin, a profoundly original inventor within the limitations of a classical ideal. He too spent most of his life in Rome though the art he created was not specifically Italian, but French. For more than two centuries afterwards everyone in France who felt called upon to depict the beauties of nature would think of Lorrain and study his works. Outside France it was the same; Lorrain was nowhere more admired than in England.

There is an element of mystery in the vocation of this humble and almost illiterate peasant whose knowledge of French and Italian was equally poor, and who used to inscribe on his drawings notes in a strange broken Franco-Italian. This mystery is in some way symbolic of that with which he imbued his pictures, le mystère dans la lumière. This admirable landscapist drew from within himself the greatest number of extraordinary pictures, in which all is beauty, poetry and truth.

He sometimes made from nature drawings so beautiful that several have been attributed to Poussin, but in his paintings his imagination dominates, growing in magnitude as he realised his genius. He understood by listening to Poussin and watching him paint that a sort of intellectual background would be an invaluable addition to his own imagination, visions, dreams and reveries.

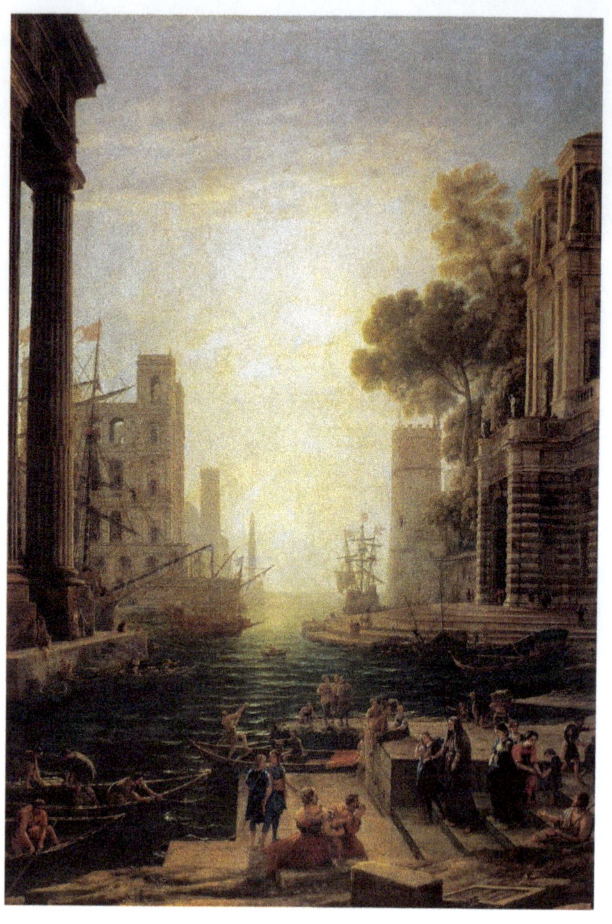

Claude Lorrain (Gellée), c. 1604-1682, ▲
Classicism, French, Embarkation of
St Paula Romana at Ostia, 1639.
Oil on canvas, 211 x 145 cm.
Museo Nacional del Prado, Madrid.

Claude Lorrain (Gellée), c. 1604-1682, ▶
Classicism, French, Landscape with Jacob, Rachel and Leah at
the Well (Morning), 1666.
Oil on canvas, 113 x 157 cm.
The State Hermitage Museum, St Petersburg.

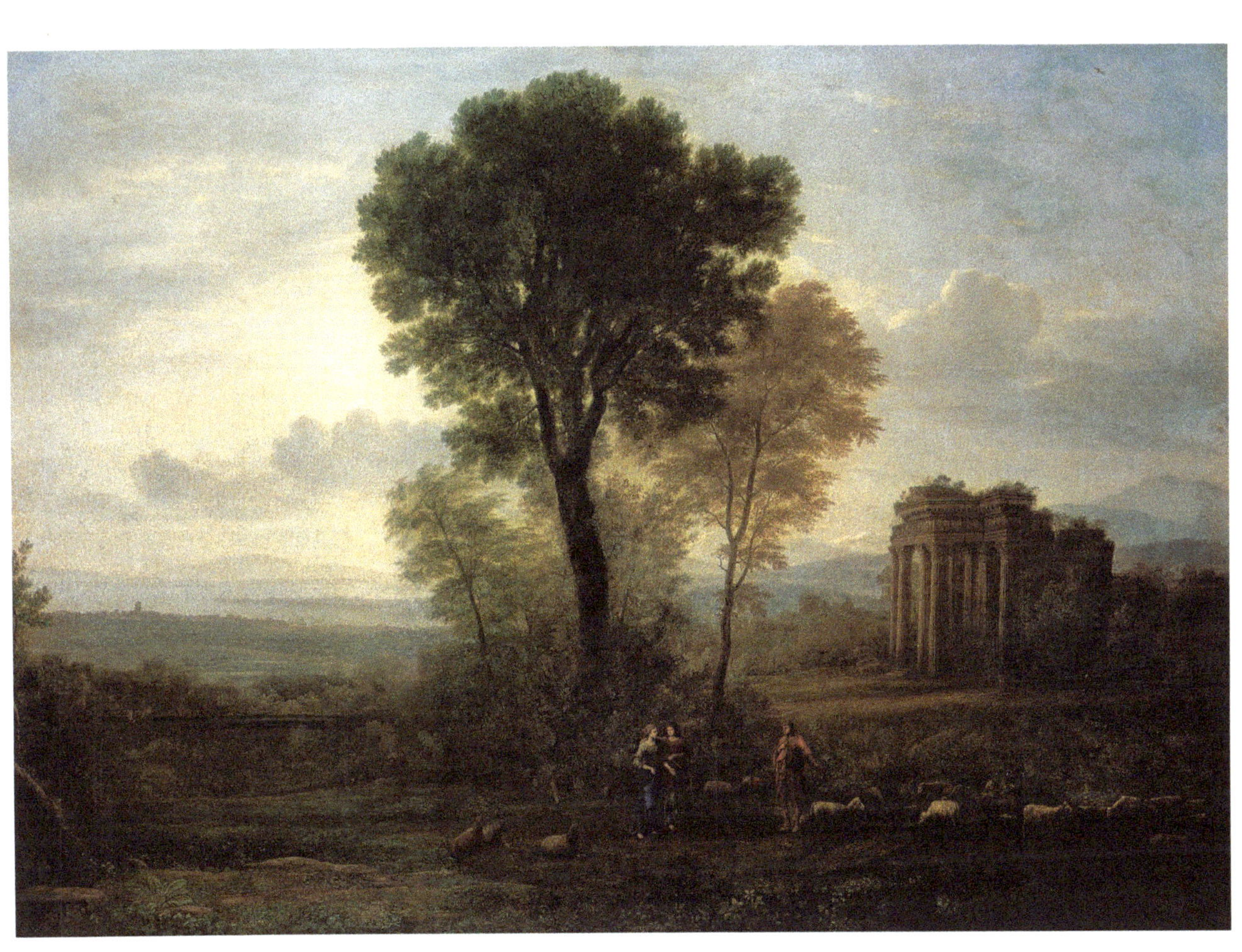

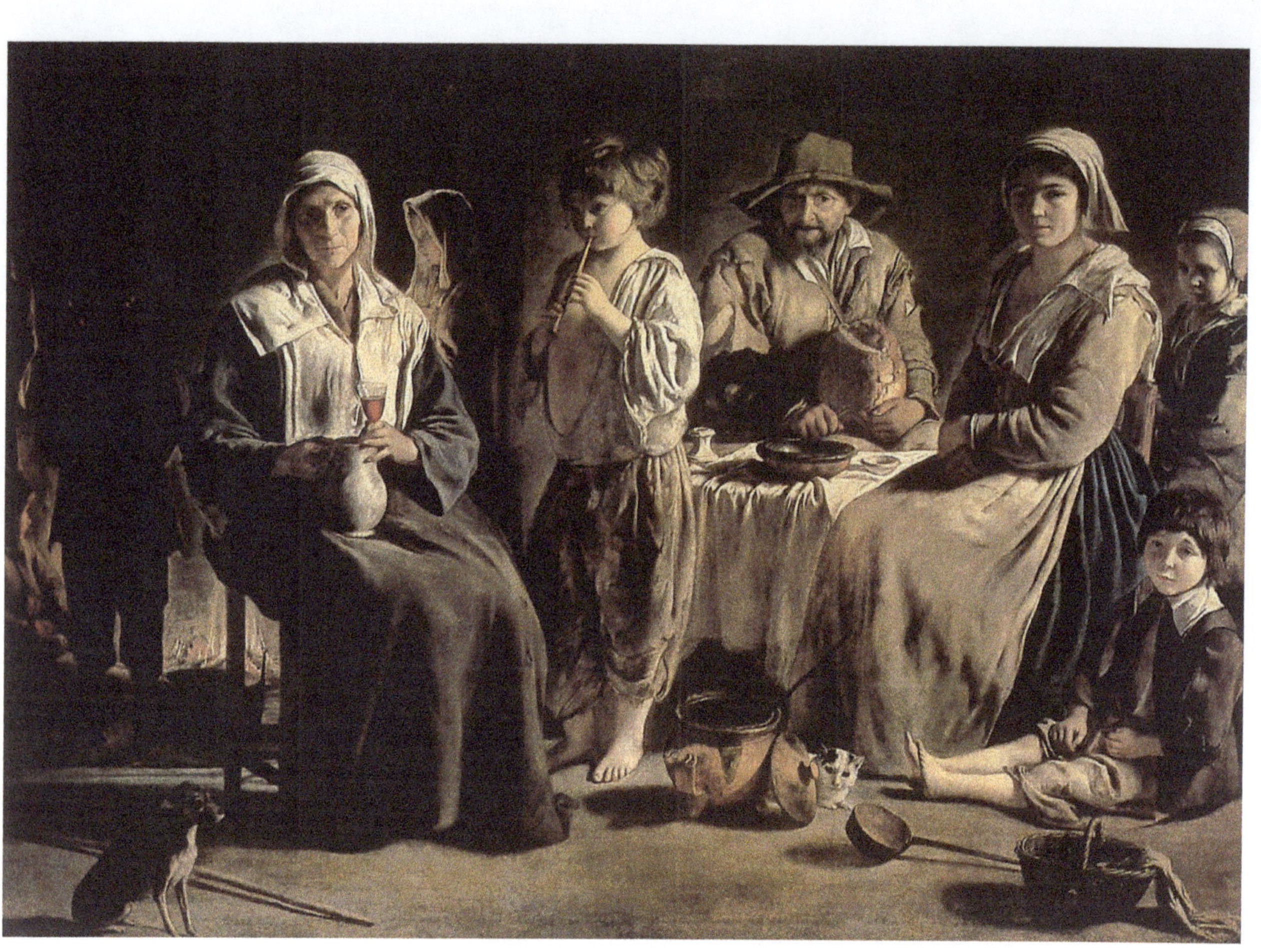

Le Nain Brothers

(Antoine C. 1600-1648, Louis c. 1598-1648 and Mathieu

c. 1607-1677 (Born in Laon, Died in Paris)

For a long time it appeared impossible to discriminate amongst the three Le Nain brothers' individual works, which have survived under their common signature. Antoine Le Nain, who studied at Laon under a 'foreign painter' (probably from Flanders), painted in a manner and with a colouring more or less derived from Flemish models; little panels where people are assembled in modest interiors, but of the town rather than of the country. His style was still slightly archaic, but it is already possible to discern in him that love of humble truth. It was from his style the inspiration for the most original works bearing the signature derived: those of Louis, the man of genius and the breaker of new ground. It was he who produced the gatherings of peasants, which are painted with such freedom, and filled with such dignity, sobriety and humanity. Contrast these with the very different treatments of similar subjects by contemporary Spanish and Italian followers of Caravaggio, on the one hand, and the Flemish and Dutch on the other. Mathieu, the youngest of the brothers, survived the others by almost thirty years. His works generally possess less depth, but he painted family gatherings in which he showed himself almost as good a judge of human physiognomy and expression as his brother Louis.

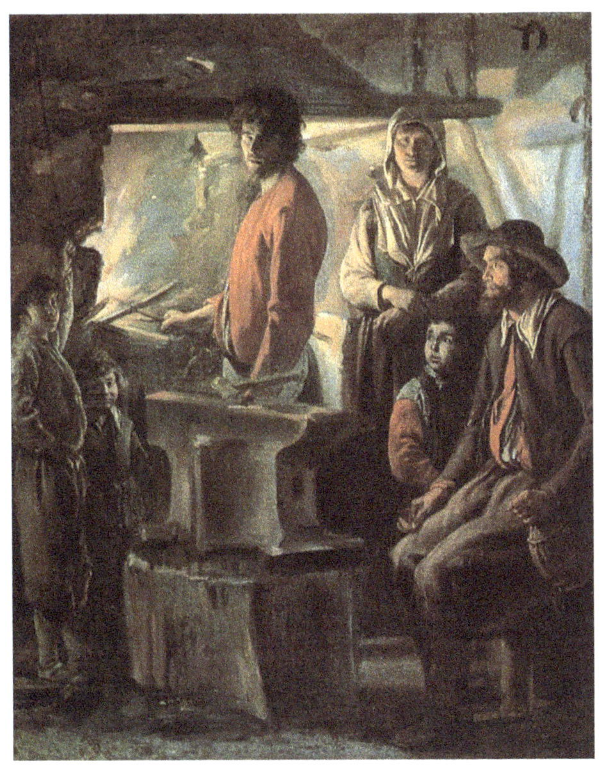

▲ **Antoine Le Nain**, c. 1600-1648,
Baroque, French, Blacksmith at his Forge, c. 1640.
Oil on canvas, 69 x 57 cm.
Musée du Louvre, Paris.

◀ **Louis Le Nain**, c. 1598-1648,
Baroque, French, Family of Country People, 1640.
Oil on canvas, 113 x 159 cm.
Musée du Louvre, Paris.

Georges de la Tour

(1593 Vic sur Ville – 1652 Lunéville)

Georges de La Tour was well known in his own time but then forgotten until the twentieth century. His painting depicted genre and religious subjects, often seen in candlelight, such as his interior scenes. The influence of Caravaggio is evident in his painting, especially in the use of chiaroscuro. Simplification of form and rigour of composition in his work underlined the ideas of the Counter-Reformation.

Georges de La Tour, ▶
Magdalene of the Night Light, c. 1640-1645.
Oil on canvas, 128 x 94 cm.
Musée du Louvre, Paris.

Georges de La Tour, 1593-1652, Baroque, French, ▼
The Card-Sharp with the Ace of Diamonds, 1635.
Oil on canvas, 106 x 146 cm.
Musée du Louvre, Paris.

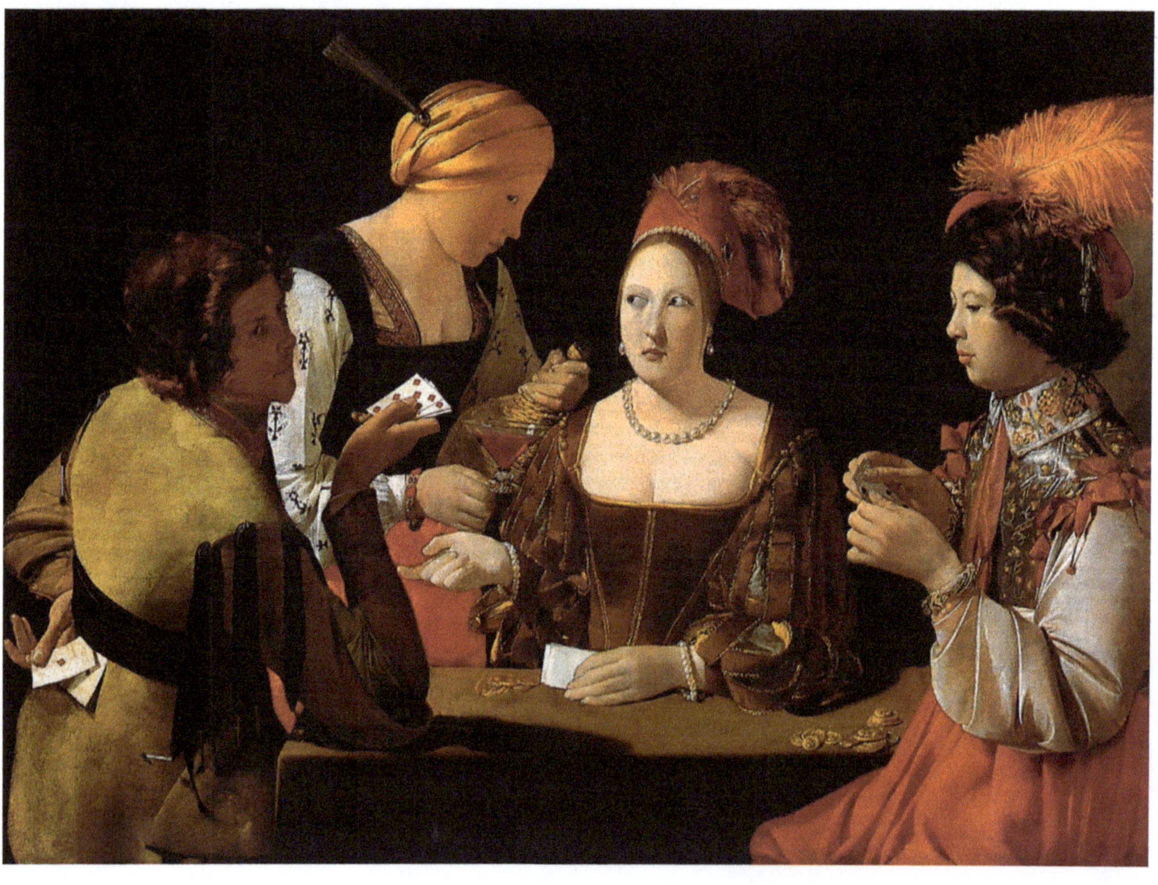

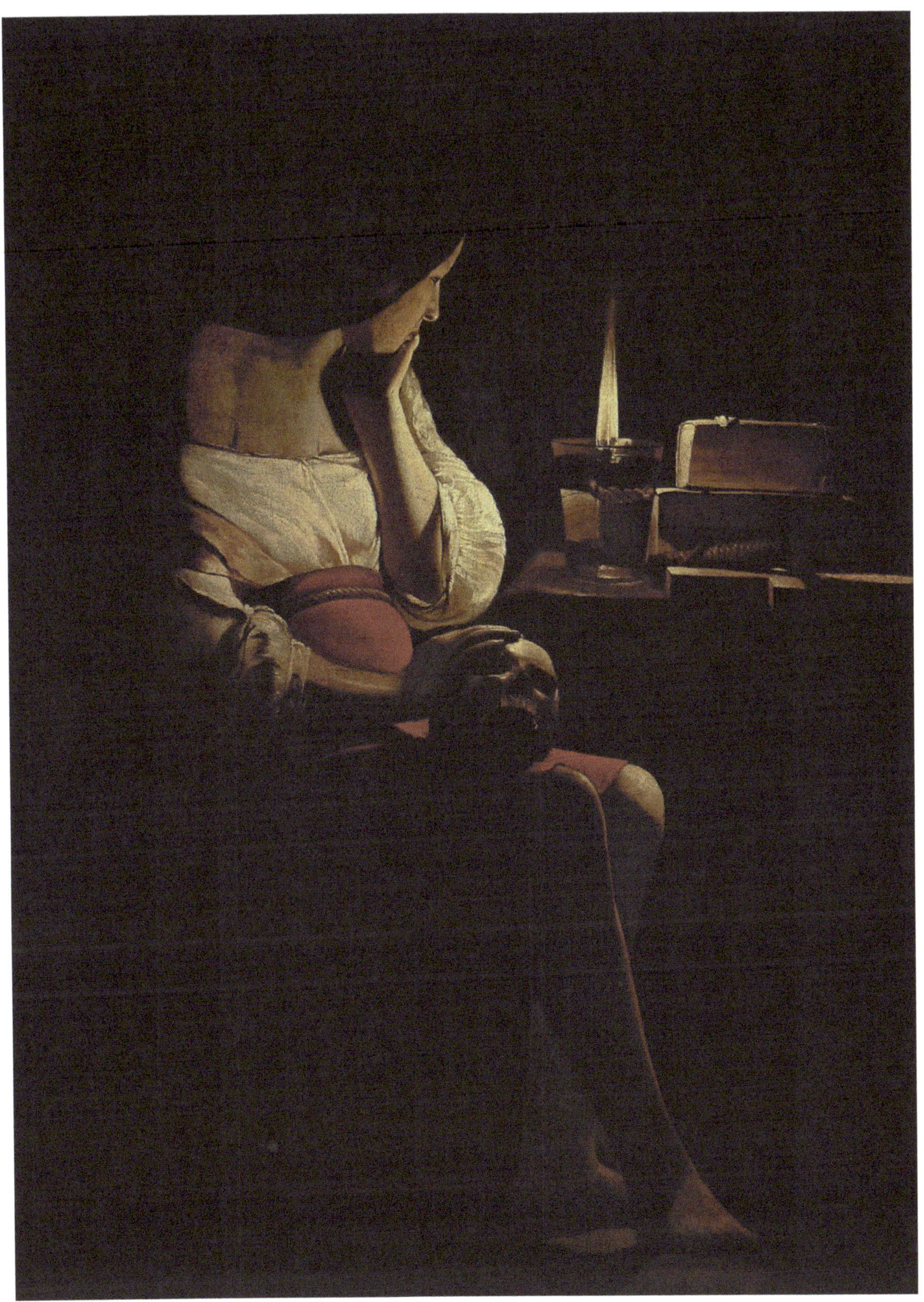

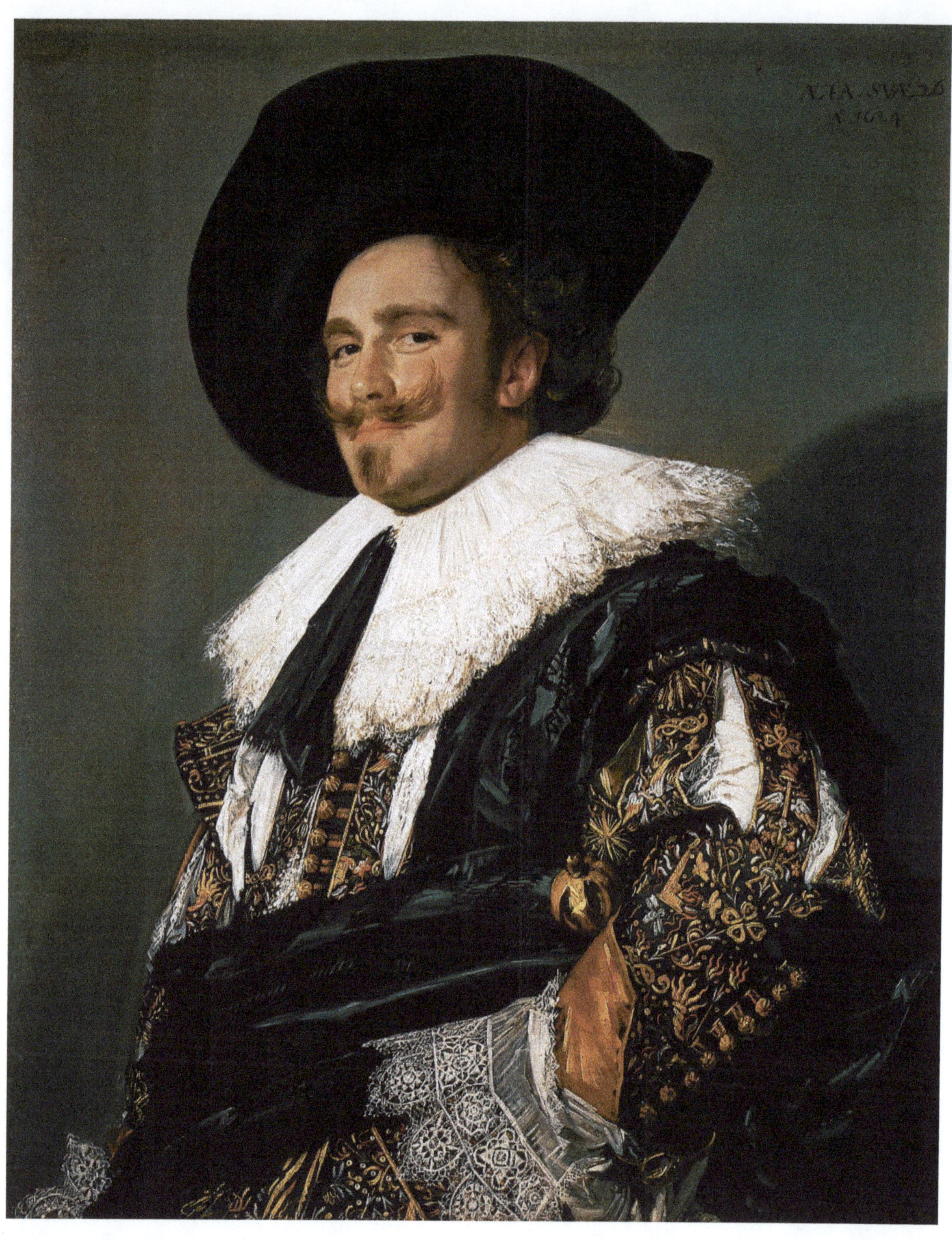

▲ **Frans Hals**, *The Laughing Cavalier*, 1624.
Oil on canvas, 83 x 67.3 cm. The Wallace Collection, London.

THE NETHERLANDS

Frans Hals

(Antwerp 1580 – Haarlem)

As a portrait painter, Frans Hals was second only to Rembrandt in Holland, he displayed extraordinary talent and quickness in the exercise of his art coupled with improvidence in the use of the means which that art secured to him. At a time when the Dutch nation fought for independence and won it, Hals appears in the ranks of its military gilds. But as a man he had failings. He so ill-treated his first wife, Anneke Hermansz, that she died prematurely in 1616; and he barely saved the character of his second, Lysbeth Reyniers, by marrying her in 1617. Another defect was partiality to drink.

Still he brought up and supported a family of ten children until 1652, when the forced sale of his pictures and furniture, at the suit of a baker to whom he was indebted for bread and money brought him to absolute penury. We may admire the spirit which enabled him to produce some of his most striking works in these unhappy circumstances.

Hals's pictures illustrate the various strata of society into which his misfortunes led him. His banquets or meetings of officers and guildsmen are the most interesting of his works. But they are not more characteristic than his low-life pictures of itinerant players and singers. His portraits of gentlefolk are true and noble, but hardly as expressive as those of fishwives and tavern heroes.

Hals was fond of daylight and silvery sheen. Both, Rembrandt and Hals were painters of touch, but of touch on different keys – Rembrandt was the bass, Hals the treble. The latter is perhaps more expressive than the former. He seizes with rare intuition a moment of life of his sitters.

In every form of his art we can distinguish his earlier style from that of later years. The earliest works that have come down to us Two Boys Playing and Singing and Banquet of the Officers of the St. Hadrian Guild (1627) exhibit him as a careful draughtsman capable of great finish, yet spiritual withal. His flesh, less clear than it becomes afterwards, is pastose and burnished. Later he becomes more effective, displays more freedom of hand and a greater command of effect. At this period we note the beautiful full-

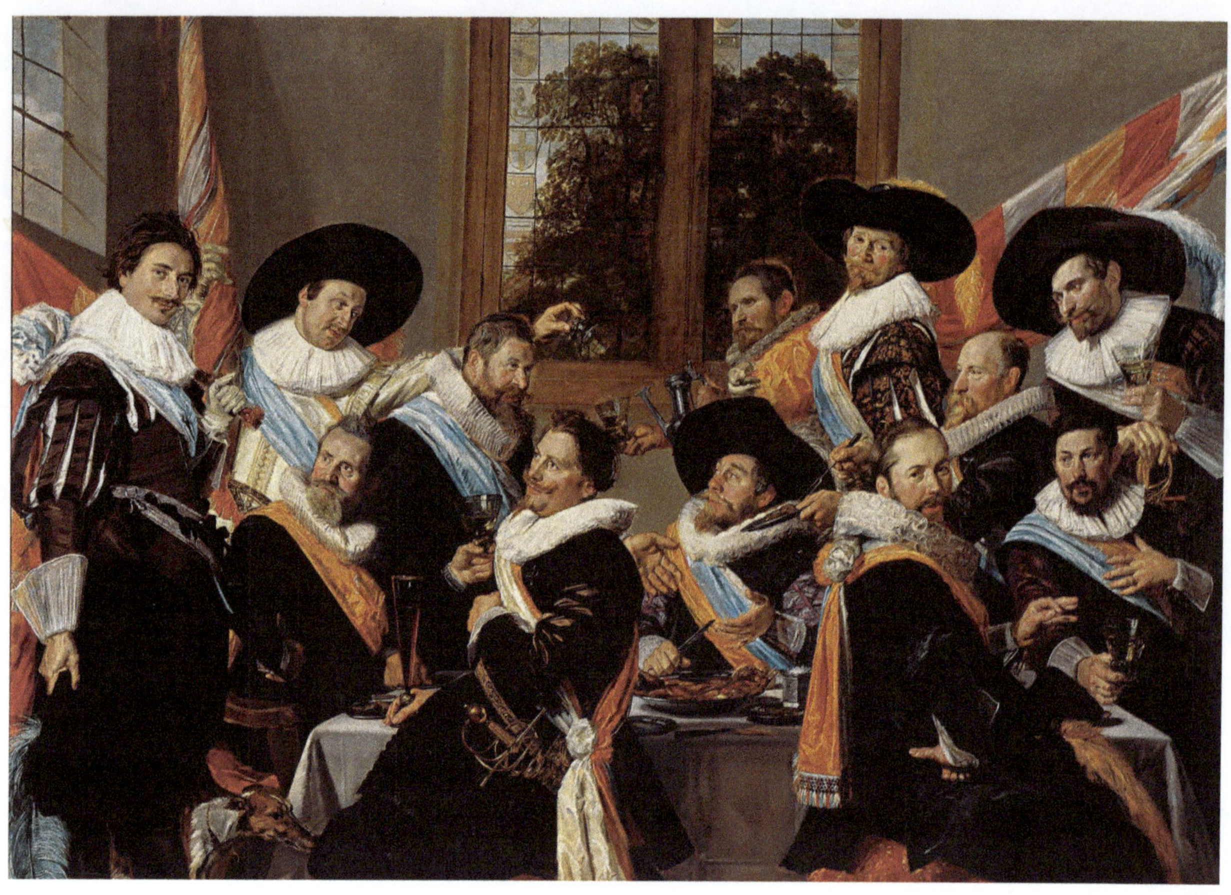

length of Madame van Beresteyn. A picture in the town hall of Amsterdam suggests some study of Rembrandt. But Rembrandt's example did not create a lasting impression on Hals. He gradually dropped more and more into grey and silvery harmonies of tone. In fact, ever since 1641 Hals had shown a tendency to restrict the gamut of his palette, and to suggest colour rather than express it.

He was, however, so shiftless that in his old age he was dependent upon the city government for support. That he received it, however, and that his creditors were lenient with him, seems to show that his contemporaries recognised greatness behind his intemperance and improvidence; and, when in his eighty-second year he died, he was buried beneath the choir of the Church of St Bavon in Haarlem.

For a long time after his death, Hals was thought little of, even in Holland, where artists forsook the traditions of their own school and went in search of other mentors – to wit, those of the Italian "grand style". It was not until well into the nineteenth century that artists returning to the truth of nature, discovered that Hals had been one of the greatest seers of the truth and one of its most virile interpreters. Today he is honoured for these qualities, and of all the much-admired Dutch pictures of the seventeenth century, his are the most characteristic of the Dutch race and of the art which it produced.

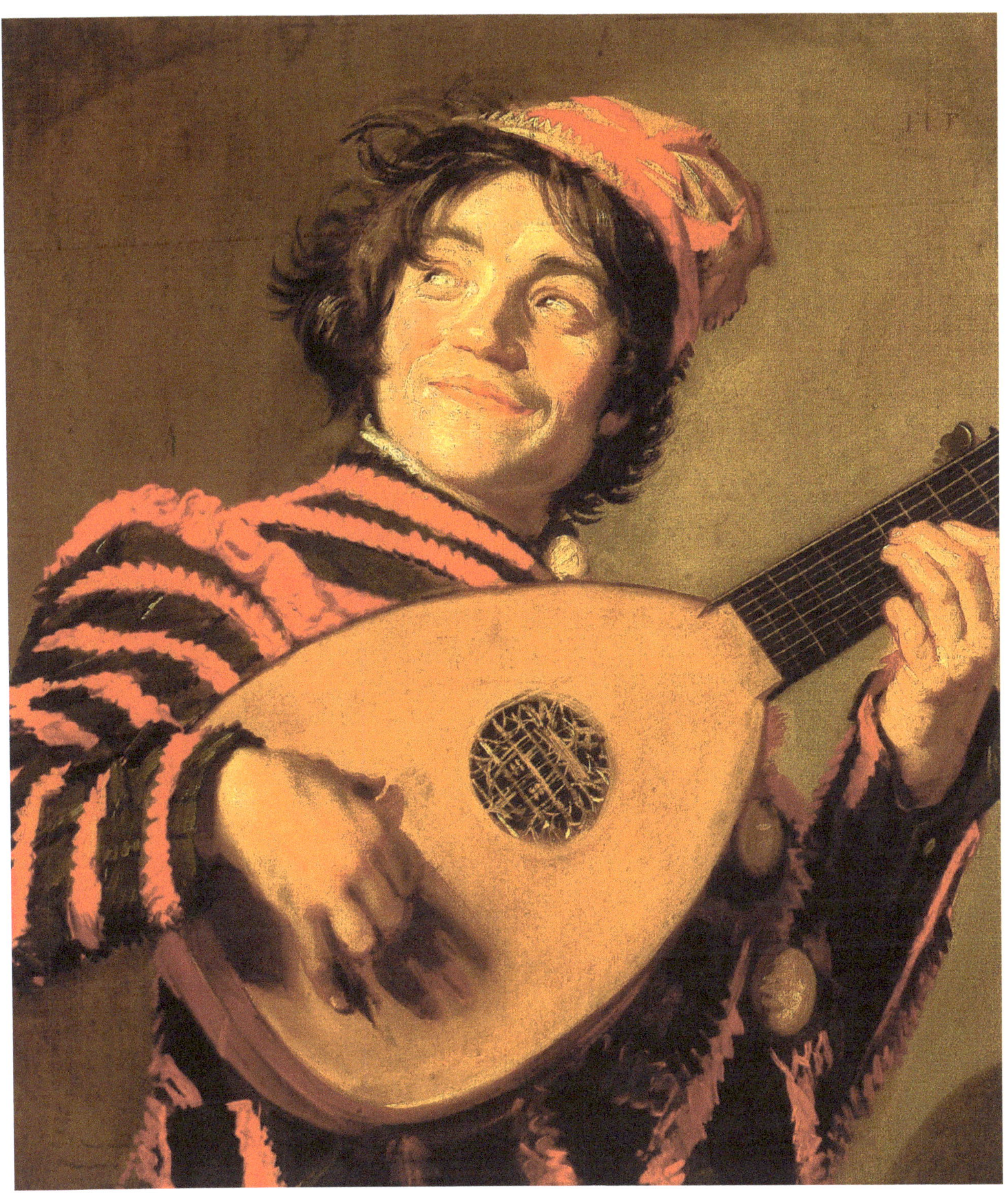

◀ **Frans Hals**, *Banquet of the Officers of the Civic Guard of St. Adrian (the Cluveniers)*, 1627.
Oil on canvas, 183 x 266.5 cm. Frans Hals Museum, Haarlem.

▲ **Frans Hals**, *Buffoon with a Lute*, c. 1624-1626.
Oil on canvas, 70 x 62 cm. Musée du Louvre, Paris.

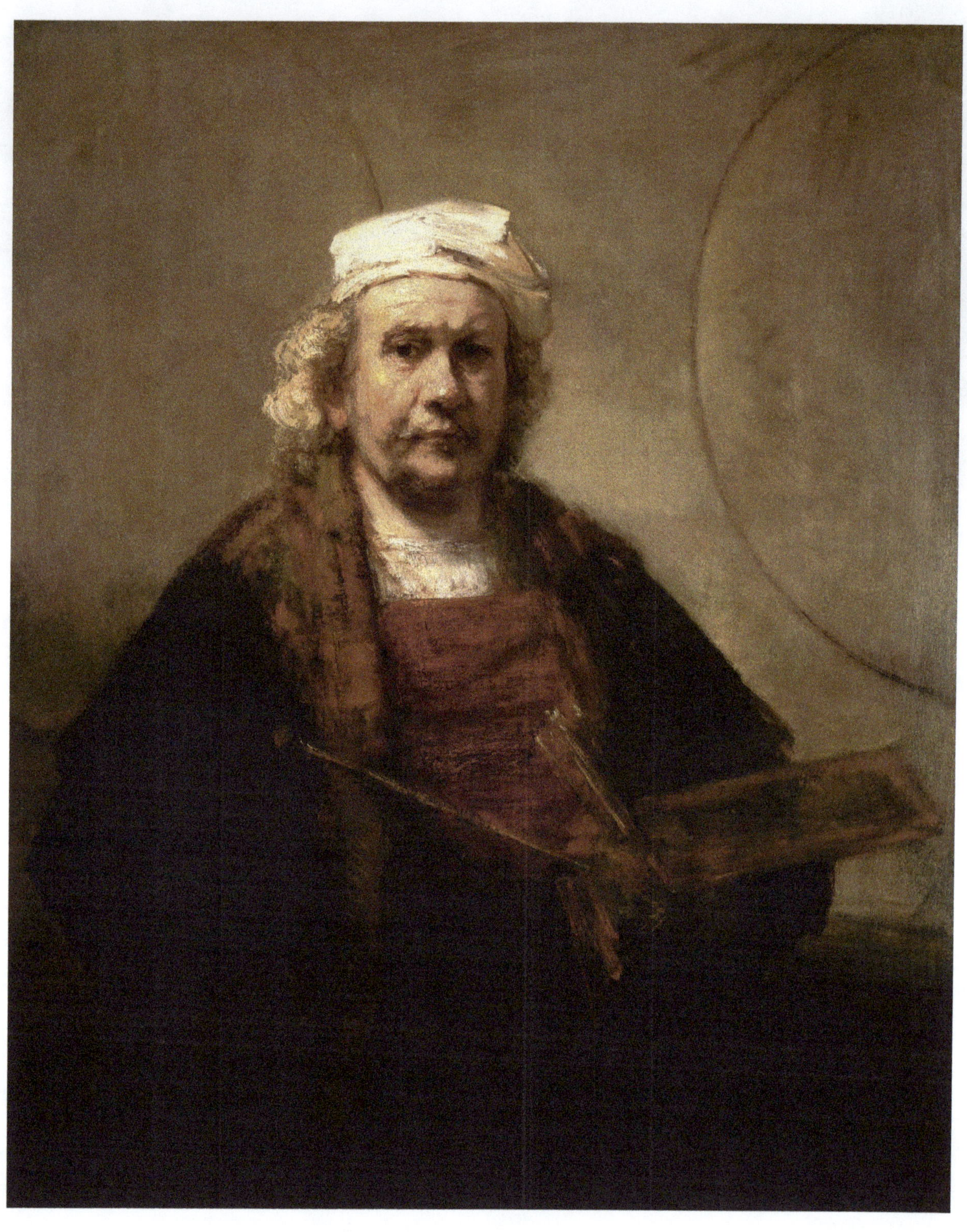

▲ **Rembrandt van Rijn**, *Self-Portrait*, 1665 (?).
Oil on canvas, 114.3 x 94 cm. Kenwood House, London.

Rembrandt (Rembrandt Harmensz Van Rijn)

(1606 Leyde – 1669 Amsterdam)

Rembrandt was born at No. 3 Weddesteg, on the rampart at Leiden overlooking the Rhine. He was the fourth son of Gerrit Harmens van Rijn, a well-to-do miller. His parents resolved that he should enter a learned profession. With this view he was sent to the High School at Leiden; but the boy soon manifested his dislike of the prospect, and determined to be a painter. During the early years of his life at Leyden Rembrandt seems to have devoted himself entirely to studies, painting and the people around him, the beggars and cripples, every picturesque face and form he could get hold of. Nine pictures are known to belong to these years, among which Presentation in the Temple. The prevailing tone of all these pictures is a greenish grey, the effect being somewhat cold and heavy. The first important work executed by Rembrandt in Amsterdam is Simeon in the Temple, a fine early example of his treatment of light and shade and of his subtle colour.

His work was now attracting the attention of lovers of art of Amsterdam. In the life-sized Lesson in Anatomy of 1632 we have the first of the great portrait subjects. It is a great picture by the grouping of the expressive portraits and by the completeness of the conception. The colour is quiet and the handling of the brush timid and precise, while the light and the shade are somewhat harsh and abrupt. The year 1634 is especially remarkable as that of Rembrandt's marriage with the beautiful fair-haired Saskia van Uylenburgh, the daughter of a Burgomaster. Till her death in 1642 she was the centre of his life and art, and lives for us in her own portraits. On her the painter lavished his magical power, painting her as the Queen Artemisia or Bathsheba and as the wife of Samson – covering her with pearls and gold. The happiness of a man who has found an adequate wife is evident in his Self-Portrait with Saskia in which he, his wife on his arm, lifts a glass to toast the viewer.

The life of Samson supplied many subjects in these early days. The greatest of this series is The Marriage of Samson. Here Rembrandt gives the rein to his imagination and makes the scene live before us. Except the bride (Saskia) who sits calm and grand on a dais in the centre of the feast, all is animated and full of bustle. In execution it is a great advance on former subject pictures; we have here signs of his approaching love of warmer tones of red and yellow.

The fact that the Old Testament in its choice of material had a greater appeal than the New Testament may be attributed to the ample study material found in the Jewish Quarter of Amsterdam, for here Rembrandt found everything that he needed for inspiration. He was especially attracted to the story of Samson, which was the inspiration for some of the most beautiful images of this type with works like Samson threatens his Father-in-Law or Sacrifice of Manoah. The most gripping in the field of religious paintings, however, was a series of five small paintings, depicting the sufferings of Christ Erection of the Cross, the Descent from the Cross, the Entombment of Christ, and the Resurrection.

Year 1642 is remarkable for Rembrandt's greatest work, which marks the zenith of Dutch painting, known as The Night Watch, in which twenty-nine life-sized civic guards are introduced issuing pell-mell from their club house. The scene is full bustle and movement. The dominant colour is the citron-yellow uniform of the musketeer, the black velvet dress of the captain and the varied green of the girl and drummer, all produce a rich and harmonious effect. However, this disorderly composition, which was only selected for the colouristic effect, was contrary to the wishes of the commissioners who demanded, above all, more ceremony for the staging of their honourable and worthy personalities as well as more pose and above all, more dignity. This picture was considered a failure for Rembrandt and for a long time nobody thought of commissioning a guild or Regent picture from him again.

But this year of great achievement was also the year of his great loss, for Saskia died in 1642. With her death his life and art was changed. There is a pathetic sadness in his pictures of the Holy Family – a favourite subject at this period of his life. With this tragedy his life lost its anchor. In 1650, his financial position went into a decline and, although he took on more portrait commissions, the ruin could not be overcome; in 1655 he declared bankruptcy and had to agree in the following year to the auctioning of his house and its valuables. He did not end up in complete poverty; he was given protection from his creditors and was still able to enjoy relatively quiet twilight years.

The street in which he lived was full of Dutch and Portuguese Jews. He accepted or invented their turbans and local dress as characteristic of the people. But in his religious pictures, it is not the costume we look at; what strikes us is the profound perception of the sentiment of the story, making them true to all time and independent of local circumstances. A notable example of this feeling is to be found in the Woman taken in Adultery.

Rembrandt touched no side of art without setting his mark on it, whether in still life, as in his dead birds or the Slaughtered Ox or in his drawings of elephants and lions. But at this period of his career we come upon a branch of his art, the landscape. One of the earliest pure landscapes known to us from Rembrandt's hand is Winter Scene, silvery and delicate. As a rule in his painted landscapes, he aims at grandeur and poetical effect.

Rembrandt van Rijn, ▶
Portrait of Saskia, c. 1635.
Oil on wood, 99.5 x 78.8 cm.
Staatliche Museum, Gemäldegalerie Alte Meister, Kassel.

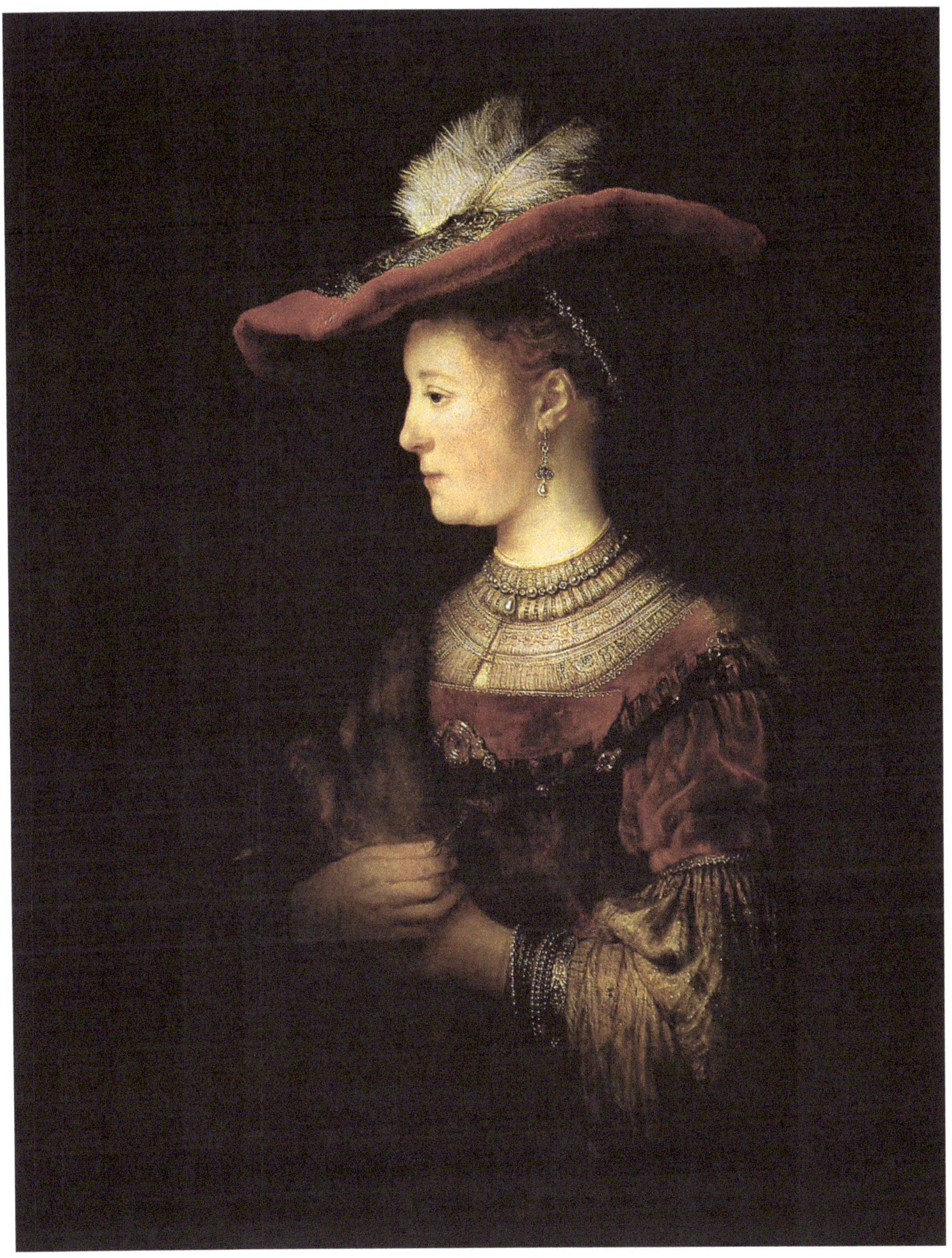

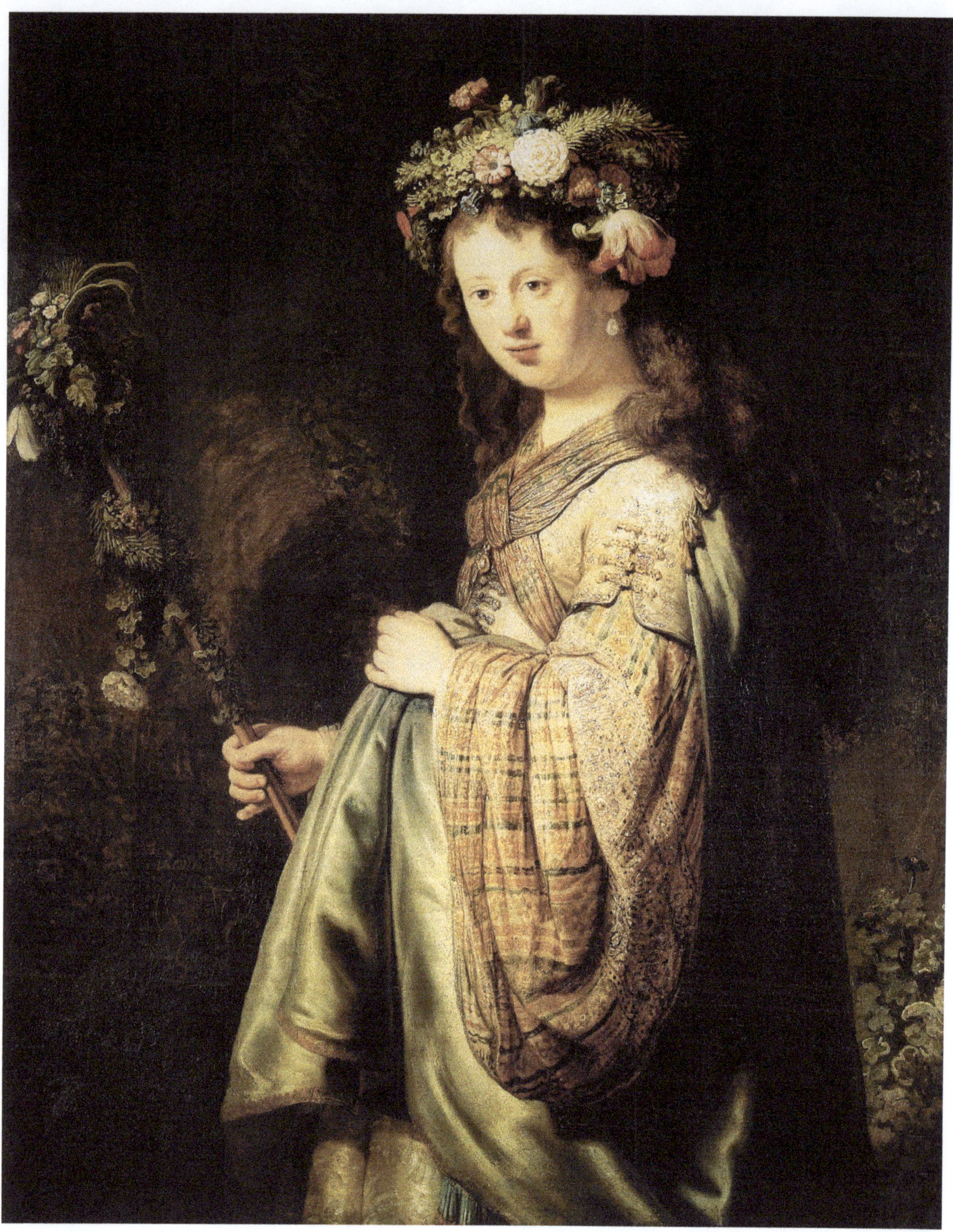

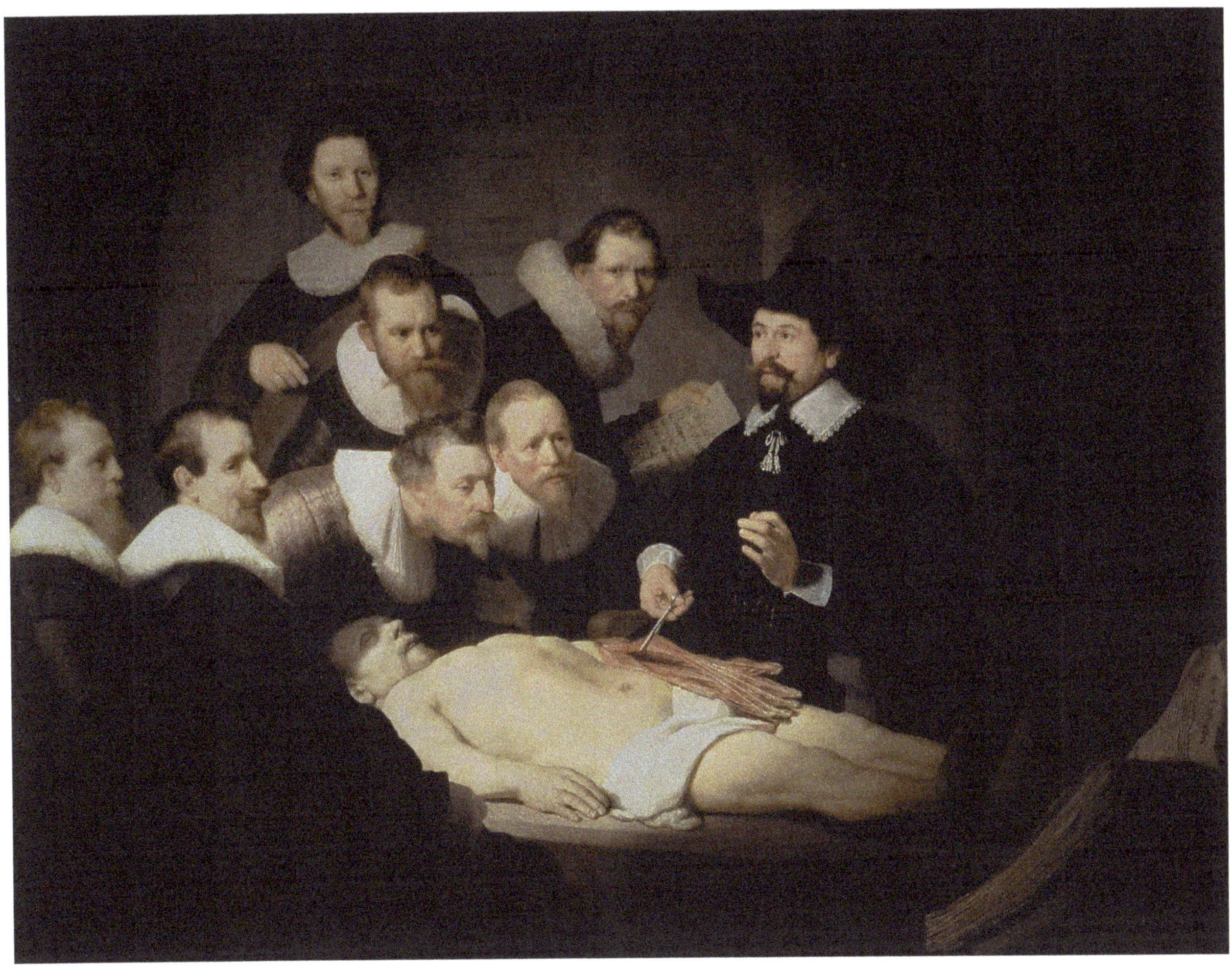

But evil days were at hand. Saskia's means were tied up in his house and we find Rembrandt borrowing considerable sums of money on the security of his house. In this year of 1654, we find Rembrandt involved in the scandal of having a child by his servant Hendrickje Stoffiels. He recognized the child and gave it the name of Cornelia, after his much-loved mother.

About the year 1663 Rembrandt painted the so-called Jewish Bride and the Family Group of Brunswick,the last and perhaps the most brilliant works of his life, bold and rapid in execution and marvelous in the subtle mixture and play of colours. In 1668 Titus, the only son of Rembrandt, died and on the 8th of October 1669, the great painter himself passed away and was buried in the Wester Kerk.

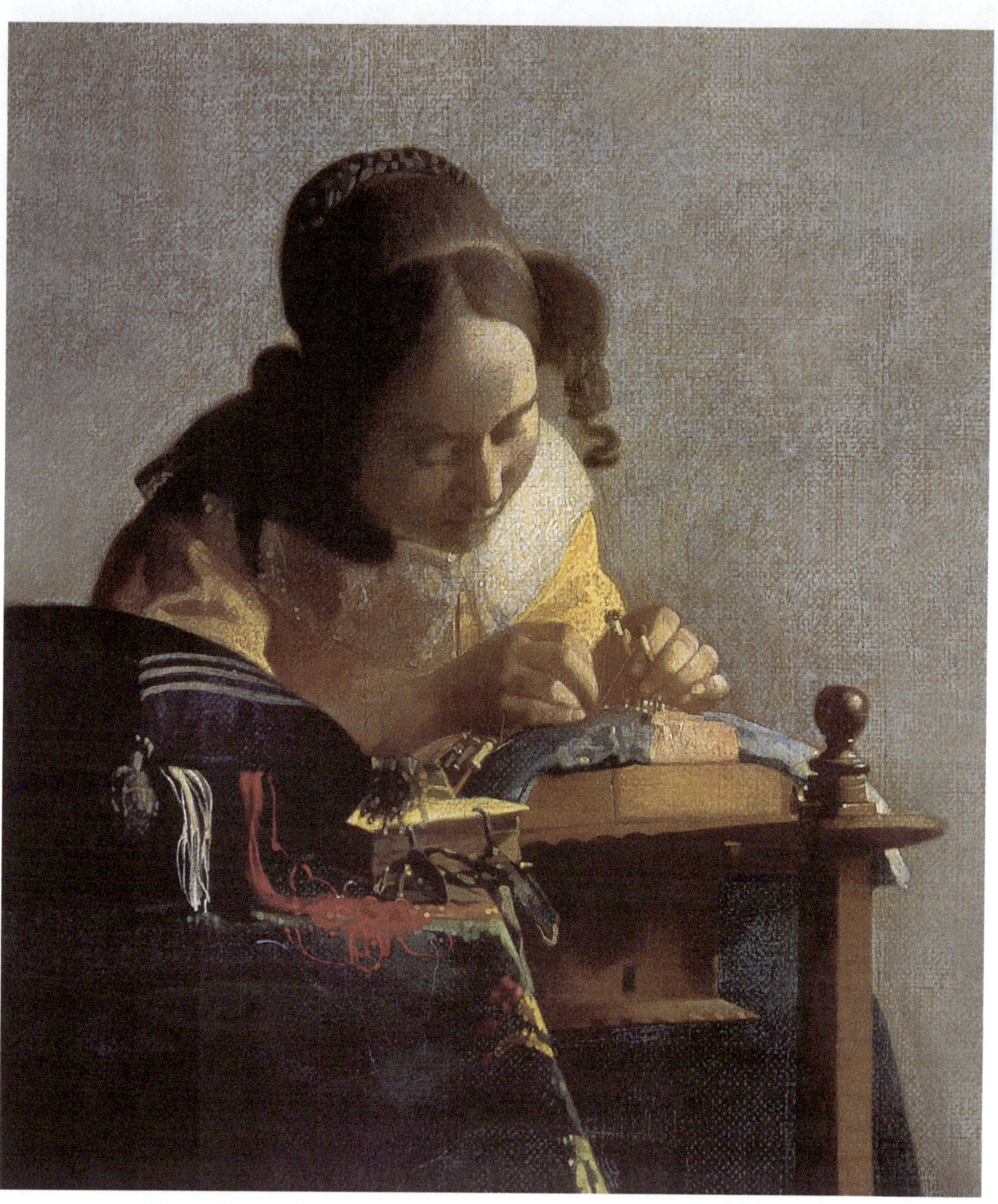

Johannes Vermeer Van Delft

(1632 – 1675 Delft)

One of the most highly appreciated artists of this period is Johannes Vermeer. He spent his whole life in his home town, where he was a pupil of Carel Fabritius, who had only come to Delft in 1650 and who was himself a pupil of Rembrandt's. Johannes Vermeer painted not only interior rooms with figures and furnishings but also the streets of Delft. Vermeer's use of lighting of interior spaces is softer than that of his predecessors, and his figures are also adapted to this type of toning: Girl reading a Letter at an open Window (1659) (p. 109), Girl with a Wine Glass (c. 1660), The Letter (after 1664), Woman with a Pearl Necklace (1665), and the studio picture The Art of Painting (c. 1666).

This last picture is taken by some experts as an allegory, sometimes called The Allegory of Painting. In any case, it is the largest and most complex of all of Vermeer's works and has an unusual history. Vermeer never sold this picture despite being up to his neck in debt. After his and his wife's death, his mother-in-law Maria Thins inherited the picture.

Then for more than a hundred years it was stored away, unrecognized and undiscovered until its purchase in 1813 by the Hungarian Count Czernin for 50 Florins. In the 1860s it was ascribed to Pieter de Hooch but was eventually recognized as a Vermeer original by a French art critic, Théophile Thoré-Bürger.

Whether this remains so is not yet certain, but in this way it gained attention and was displayed to the public in Austria in exhibitions in Vienna until the arrival of the Nazis in 1939. The leading Nazi figures, including the collection-mad former Reichsmarschall Hermann Goering, showed a strong interest in this picture; it was finally sold by its owner the Count Jaromir Czernin on the twentieth of November in 1940 to Adolf Hitler for his private collection for a price of 1,650,000 reichsmarks. During World War II it was hidden in a salt mine to protect it from allied bombardment. After the war, in 1946, the painting was handed over to the Austrian Government and is today in the possession of the Austrian State.

◀ **Johannes Vermeer**,
The Lacemaker, c. 1669-1670.
Oil on canvas, 24 x 21 cm.
Musée du Louvre, Paris.

Peter Paul Rubens

(1577 Siegen – 1640 Antwerp)

This Grand Master of Flemish painting is one of the most recognizable figures in the history of art. His father, a druggist, although of humble descent, was a man of learning and councilor and alderman in his native town. A Roman Catholic by birth, he became a zealous upholder of the Reformation. After a list of followers of the Reformed creed got into the hands of the Duke of Alva, Johannes Rubens lost no time in quitting Spanish soil, ultimately settling in Cologne with his wife and four children.

In his new residence he became legal adviser to Anne of Saxony. Before long it was discovered that their relations were not purely of a business kind. Thrown into the dungeons, Rubens lingered there for many months. He finally got leave and returned to Antwerp. Peter Paul was scarcely ten years old.

Not the slightest trace of his first master, Tobias Verhaecht's influence, can be detected in Rubens's works. Not so with Adam van Noort to whom the young man was next apprenticed, thereafter he studied under Otto van Veen, a gentleman by birth, a most distinguished Latin scholar and a painter of very high repute. From 1600 to 1608, Rubens belonged to the household of the Duke of Mantua who had his attention drawn by one of his courtiers to Rubens's genius.

Rubens came to Italy full of expectations, and full of spirit; it is easy to understand that the dramatic, forceful and passionate was more to the taste of the young man than the quiet beauty of Italian art. In Venice, Tintoretto had a much greater effect on him than Titian or Veronese. when he finally came to Rome, he marvelled at Michelangelo and Caravaggio. The latter for a time had the strongest influence on Rubens's creations, which can be recognized in works such as the triptych The Raising of the Cross in Antwerp Cathedral. At the beginning of 1603, the "The Fleming" as he was termed in Mantua, was sent to Spain with a variety of presents for Philip III. Of Rubens's abilities of that time, we get a more complete idea from the immense picture Baptism of Our Lord, originally painted for the Jesuits at Mantua.

Rubens was called back to Antwerp by the death of his mother. He left Italy reluctantly with the fixed intention of returning shortly. But, with many commissions and honours from the governing couple of the Netherlands, his work bound him to his home as did his marriage in 1609 to Isabella Brandt Self-Portrait with Isabella Brandt (1609-1610).

Peter Paul Rubens, ▶
Portrait of Susanna Lunden (?)
('Le Chapeau de Paille'), probably 1622-1625.
Oil on wood, 79 x 54.6 cm.
The National Gallery, London.

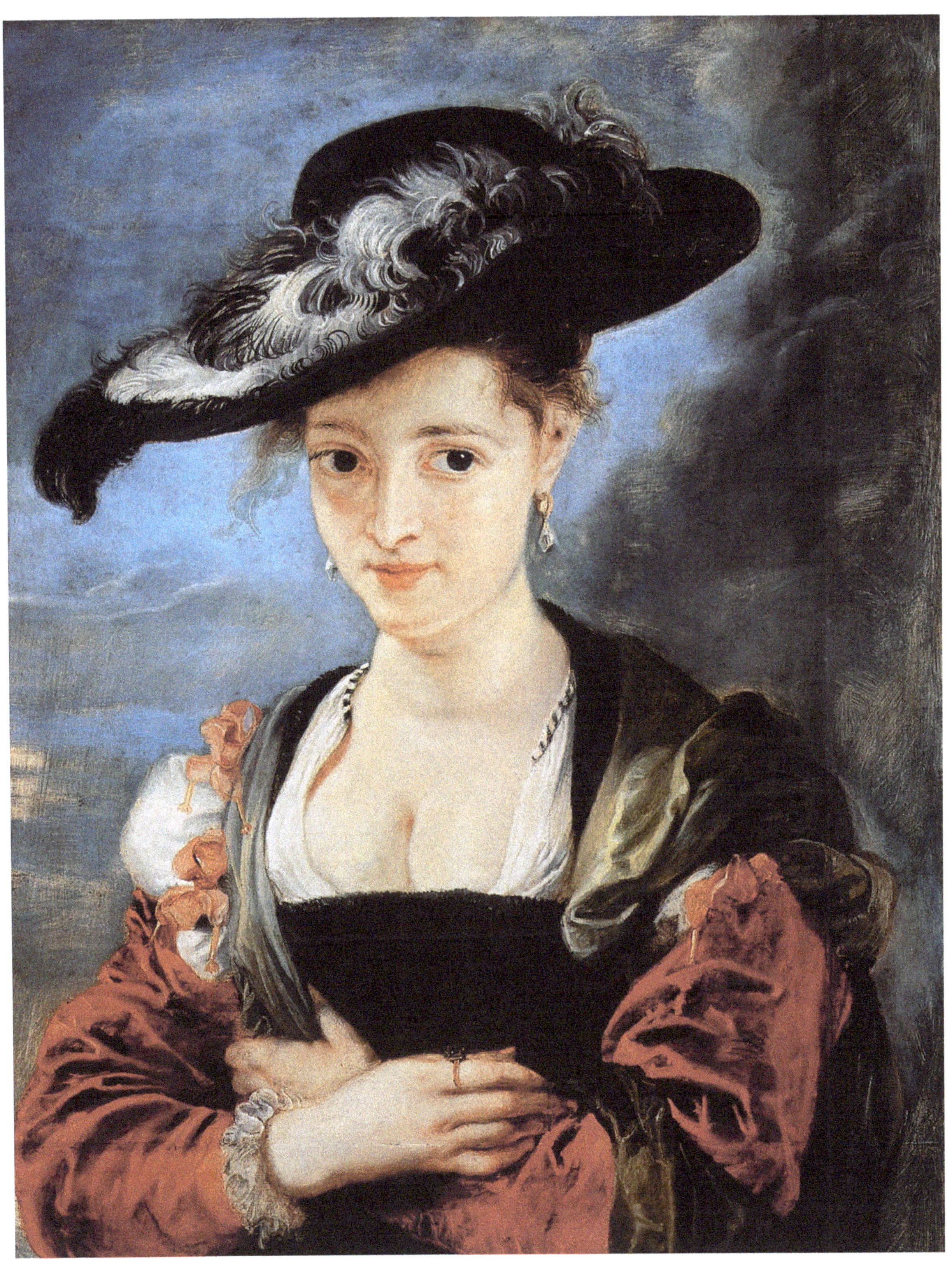

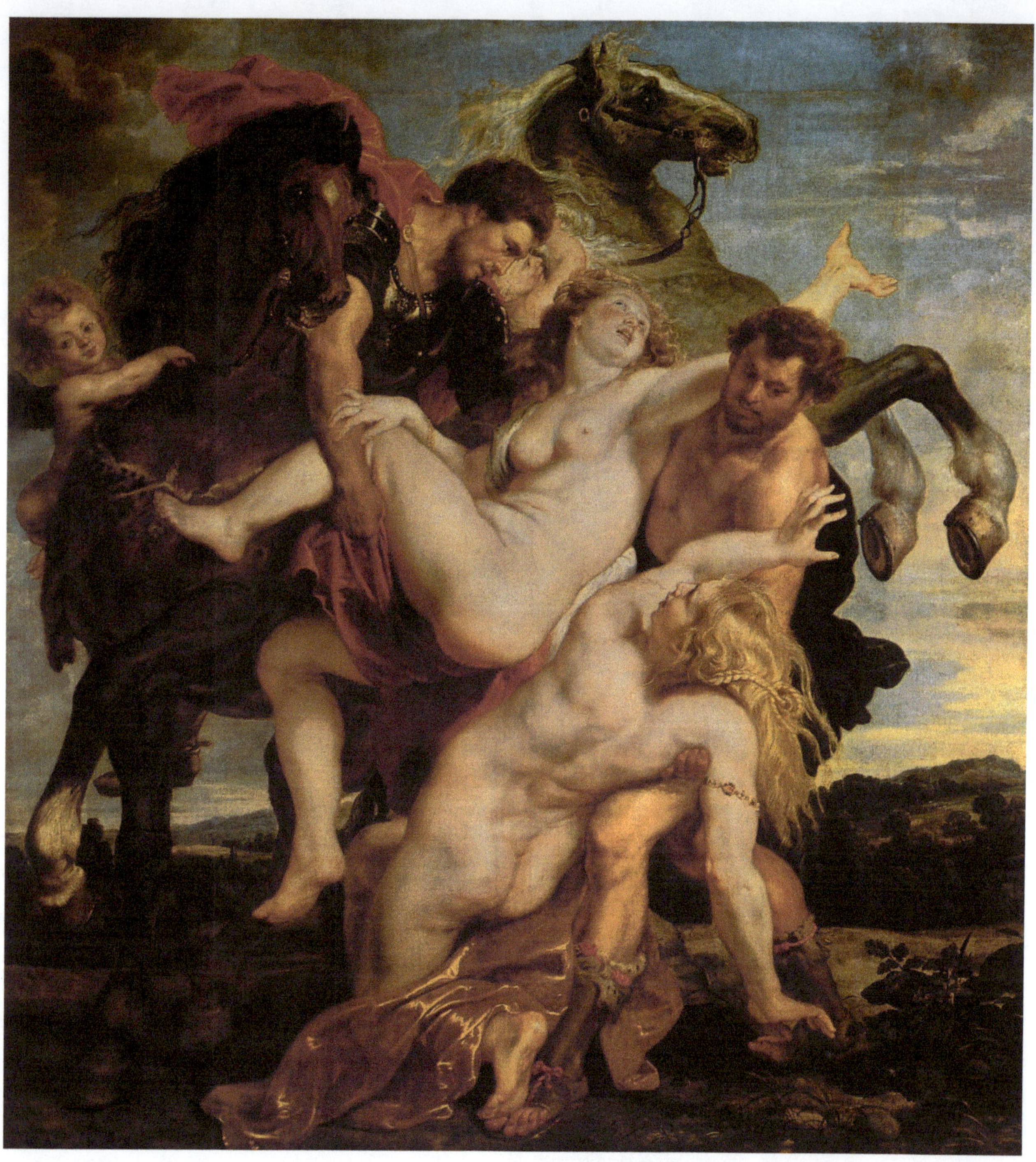

Many pictures have made us familiar with the graceful young woman who was for seventeen years to share the master's destinies. Only at the start of the 1630s, after he entered a second marriage with the 16-year-old Helena Fourment, did a new ideal of beauty appear in Rubens's art.

Rubens was uninterruptedly busy in Antwerp until 1621. In that year he undertook a journey to Paris to which he had been called by the Queen Maria de Medici, queen-mother of France in order to decorate a gallery with paintings in the Palais Luxembourg for the purpose of glorifying her life with her husband Henry IV. Rubens did not come only as a painter, but also as a diplomat. The Archduchess Isabella, sole Regent after the death of Duke Albrecht, had entrusted him with diplomatic duties, in which he was very successful.

The new Rubens style becomes noticeable for the first time in the famous Descent from the Cross (1611-1614), which demonstrates the monumental size and wholeness of the composition with its depth of perception. The dramatic, emotional movement was at the forefront of his art at the time, and it was not for nothing that he copied a section of Leonardo's cartoon Battle at Anghiari (1503). A painter who could paint such a tumult of falling human bodies and such rearing horses could also dare to compete with Michelangelo in the depiction of the Day of Judgement. As a colourist Rubens even perhaps

◄ **Peter Paul Rubens**,
The Rape of the Daughters of Leucippus, c. 1618.
Oil on canvas, 222 x 209 cm.
Alte Pinakothek, Munich.

overshadowed him. Besides Michelangelo, no other painter had such a great knowledge of the human body and at the same time so much visual power as Rubens. This knowledge of the human body inspired him especially to depict scenes from Greco-Roman mythology in which he not only satisfied his own tastes but also those of his sponsors and patrons. From an artistic point of view he created something wonderful in his works, as can easily be seen in the Robbery of the Daughters of the Leukippos.

Rubens was now fifty-three years of age; he had been four years a widower and before the end of the year (December 1630) he entered into a second marriage with a beautiful girl of sixteen, named Helena Fourment. She was an admirable model, and none of her husband's works may be more justly termed masterpieces than those in which she is represented. Once he painted her in almost life-size, half enclosed in a summer fur, a picture that became famous as The Summer Fur. Inspired more than ever by the glorious works of Titian, he now produced some of his best paintings. Could anything give a higher idea of Rubens's genius than, for example, the Feast of Venus or the St. Ildefonsus Altar?

More fortunate than many other artists, Rubens left the world in the midst of his glory. Not the remotest trace of approaching old age, not the slightest failing of mind or skill, can be detected even in his latest works, such as the Martyrdom of St. Peter, or the Judgement of Paris, where his young wife appears for the last time. Including his diplomatic correspondence, the number of letters that he wrote at this age is estimated at around six thousand, of which, unfortunately, only a small part is still in existence.

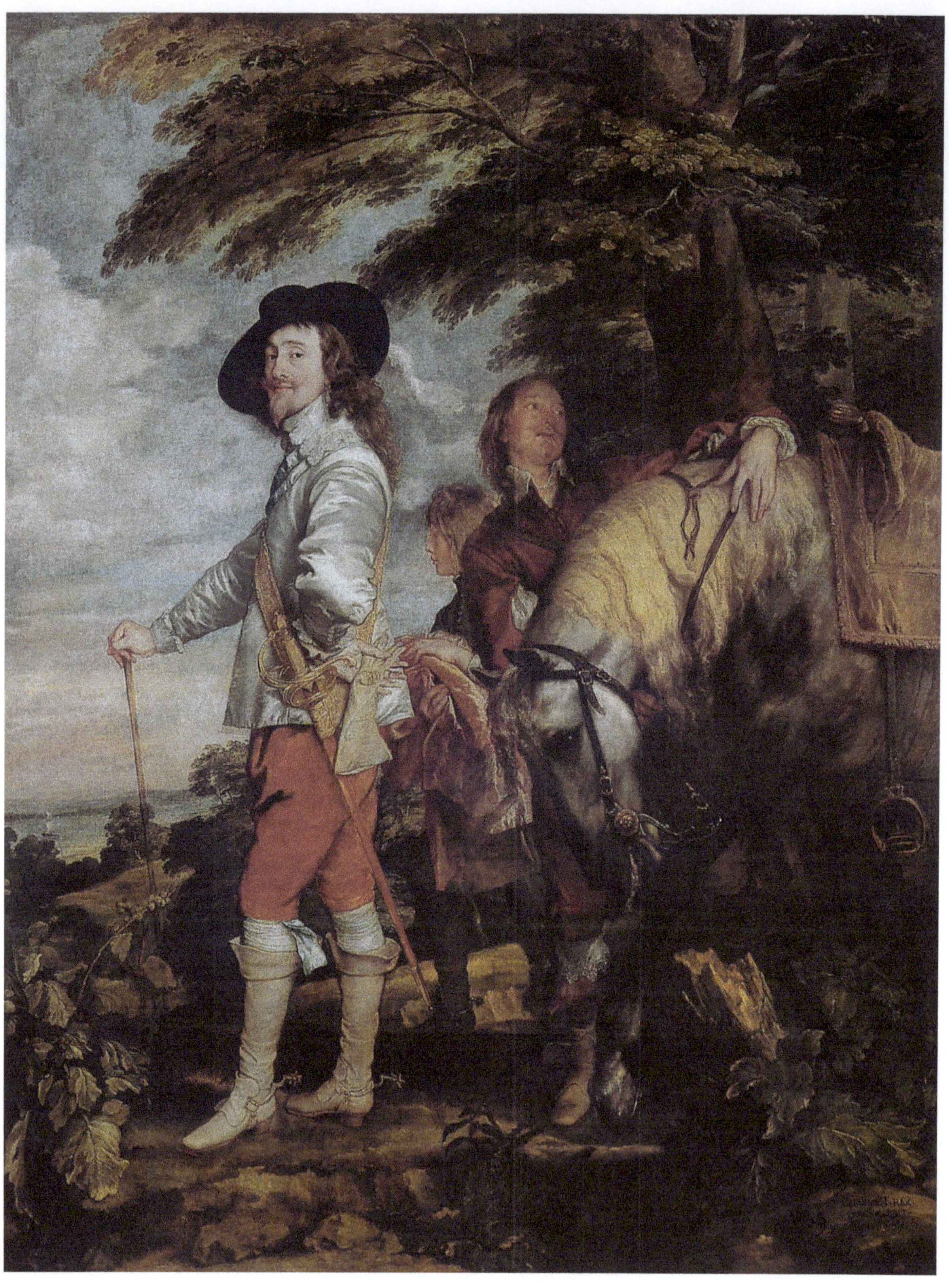

Anthony Van Dyck

(1599 Antwerp – 1641 London)

Van Dyck was accustomed early to Rubens's sumptuous lifestyle; and, when he visited Italy with letters of introduction from his master, lived in the palaces of his patrons, himself adopting such an elegant ostentation that he was spoken of as 'the Cavalier Painter'. After his return to Antwerp, his patrons belonged to the rich and noble class, and his own style of living was modelled on theirs; so that, when in 1632 he received the appointment of court painter to Charles I of England, he maintained an almost princely establishment, and his house at Blackfriars was a resort of fashion. The last two years of his life were spent travelling on the Continent with his young wife, the daughter of Lord Gowry. His health, however, had been broken by the excesses of work, and he returned to London to die. He was buried at St Paul's Cathedral.

Van Dyck tried to amalgamate the influences of Italy (Titian, Veronese, Bellini) and Flanders and he succeeded in some paintings, which have a touching grace, notably in his Madonnas and Holy Families, his Crucifixions and Depositions from the Cross, and also in some of his mythological compositions. In his younger days he painted many altarpieces full of sensitive religious feeling and enthusiasm. However, his main glory was as a portraitist, the most elegant and aristocratic ever known. The great Portrait of Charles I in the Louvre is a work unique for its sovereign elegance. In his portraits, he invented a style of elegance and refinement which became a model for the artists of the seventeenth and eighteenth centuries.

The time remaining until his death on December 9, 1641 was spent in London apart from a short trip to Paris. His comparatively early death can probably be attributed to the great stresses and efforts he required of his body.

◀ **Anthony van Dyck**,
Charles I at the Hunt, 1635.
Oil on canvas, 266 x 207 cm.
Musée du Louvre, Paris.

Pieter Brueghel the Elder

(1525 Near Breda – 1569 Brussels)

Pieter Bruegel was the first important member of a family of artists who were active for four generations. Firstly, a drawer before becoming a painter, he painted religious themes, such as Babel Tower, with very bright colours. Influenced by Hieronymus Bosch, he painted large, complex scenes of peasant life and scripture or spiritual allegories, often with crowds of subjects performing a variety of acts, yet his scenes are unified with an informal integrity and often with wit. In his work, he brought a new humanising spirit. Befriending the Humanists, Bruegel composed true philosophical landscapes in the heart of which man accepts his fate passively, caught in the track of time.

Jan I Brueghel the Elder, ▶
Bouquet, 1603.
Oil on wood, 125 x 96 cm.
Alte Pinakothek, Munich.

Pieter Bruegel the Elder, c. 1525-1569, ▼
Northern Renaissance, Flemish, Netherlandish Proverbs, 1559.
Oil on oak panel, 117 x 163 cm.
Stiftung Staatliche Museen, Gemäldegalerie, Berlin.

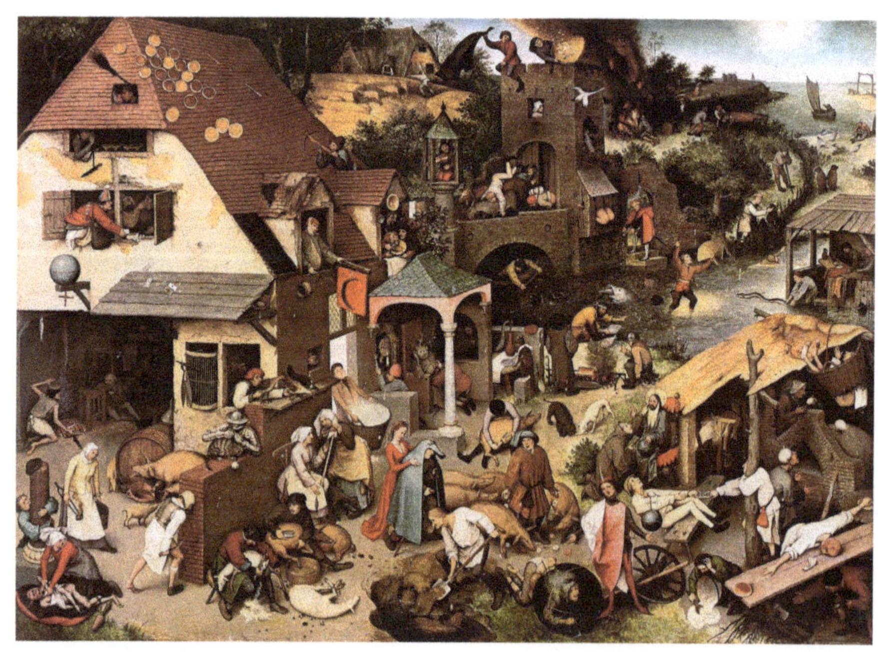

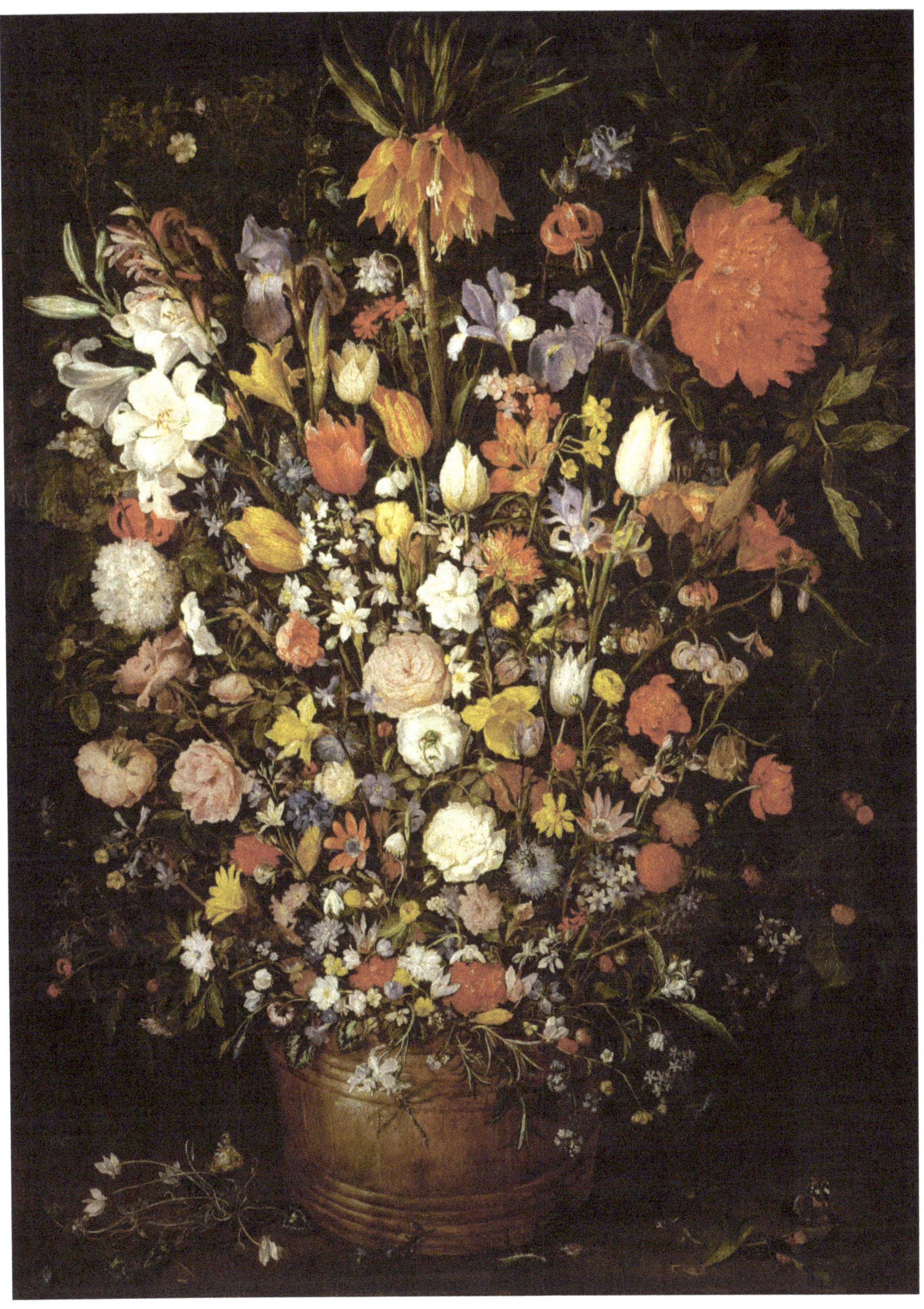

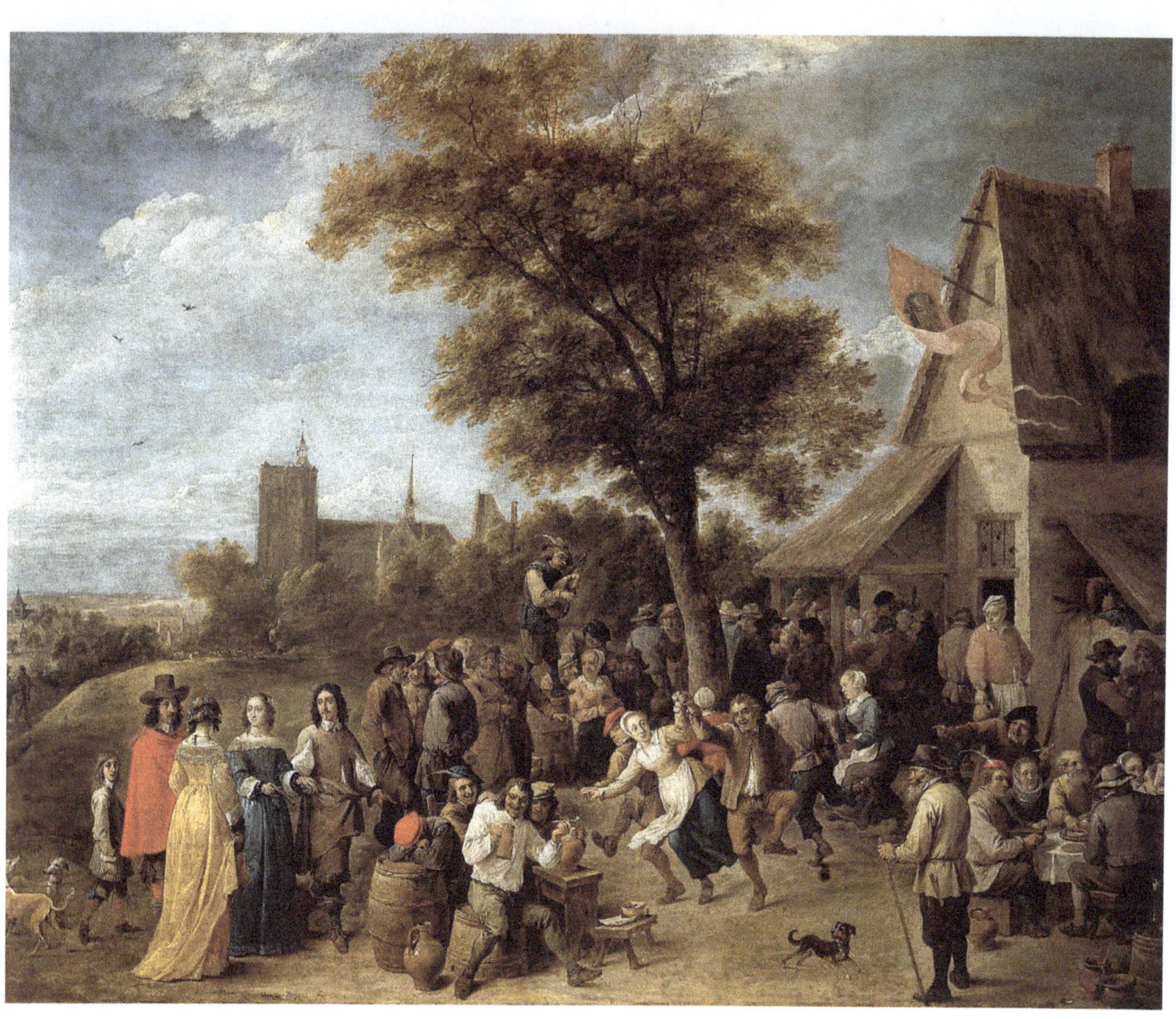

David Teniers the Younger

(1610 Antwerp– 1690 Brussels)

David Teniers the Younger was the more celebrated son of his father, almost ranking in celebrity with Rubens and Van Dyck. Through his father he was indirectly influenced by Elmsheimer and by Rubens. Anne Breughel, the daughter of John (Velvet) Breughel married Tenier in 1637.

Some really first-rate works – the Prodigal Son and Topers as well as a part of gentlemen and ladies at dinner termed the Five Senses are remarkable instances of the perfection attained by the artist when he was scarcely twenty. He was little over thirty when the Antwerp gild of St. George enabled him to paint the marvelous picture Meeting of the Civic Guards. Correct to the minutest detail, yet striking in effect, the scene under the rays of glorious sunshine, displays an astonishing amount of acquired knowledge and natural good taste.

Teniers the Younger also became the painter of the life of the common Flemish people, found in the streets and in smoky inns. His senses missed none of the corner bars in which the peasants and the other citizens came together to celebrate and carouse.

Teniers the Younger was always restrained in his inn studies, as the man who disliked excesses. In his pictures, in which he shows himself and his family in his country home, he portrays himself as the complete cavalier. But his peasant paintings were only created to keep up with the fashion. His heart was at Court, and there he served his patron the Archduke Leopold Wilhelm not only as a painter but also as an art expert. Teniers died in Brussels on the 25th of April 1690.

◄ **David Teniers the Younger**,
Peasants merrymaking, 1650.
Oil on copper, 69 x 86 cm.
Museo Nacional del Prado, Madrid.

Adriaen Brouwer

(Oudenaarde, c. 1605 – Antwerp, 1638)

Brouwer had come to the Netherlands at a young age. There he was first drafted into military service to fight against the Spaniards. In 1626 he went to Haarlem and became a pupil of Frans Hals, with whom his genius developed so quickly that he was soon able to give more to Hals than he received.

Brouwer's area of focus was the Dutch inn; he painted it and its guests with such unsurpassed truth and incomparable pictorial force that even the deviant and degrading appeared ennobled. Not only did Brouwer illustrate the individual figures of smokers and drinkers, but he also showed orgies and wild bar fights as several of his standard subjects.

Brouwer also lived the life he painted. Having moved to Antwerp in 1631, he died there in 1638, constantly hounded by his creditors. The few pictures he painted there were partly bought by artistic friends, including Rubens. A very colourful masterpiece, in which he really showed his talent, is The Brawl (c. 1630-1640).

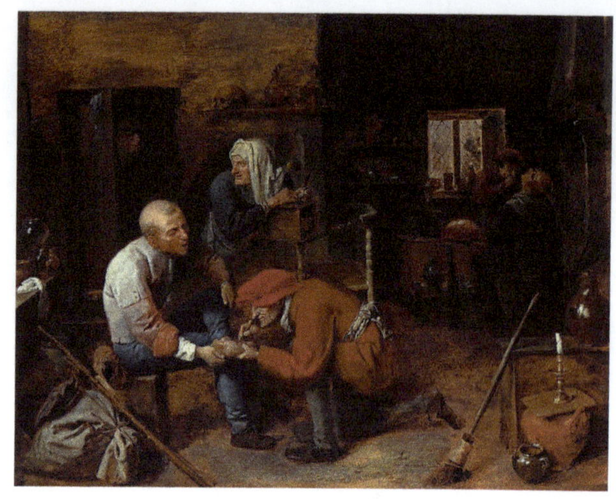

Adriaen Brouwer, 1605-1638, ▲
Baroque, Flemish, The Operation, 1631.
Oil on panel, 31.4 x 39.6 cm.
Alte Pinakothek, Munich.

Adriaen Brouwer, ▶
The Smokers, c. 1636.
Oil on canvas, 46.4 x 36.8 cm.
The Metropolitan Museum of Art, New York.

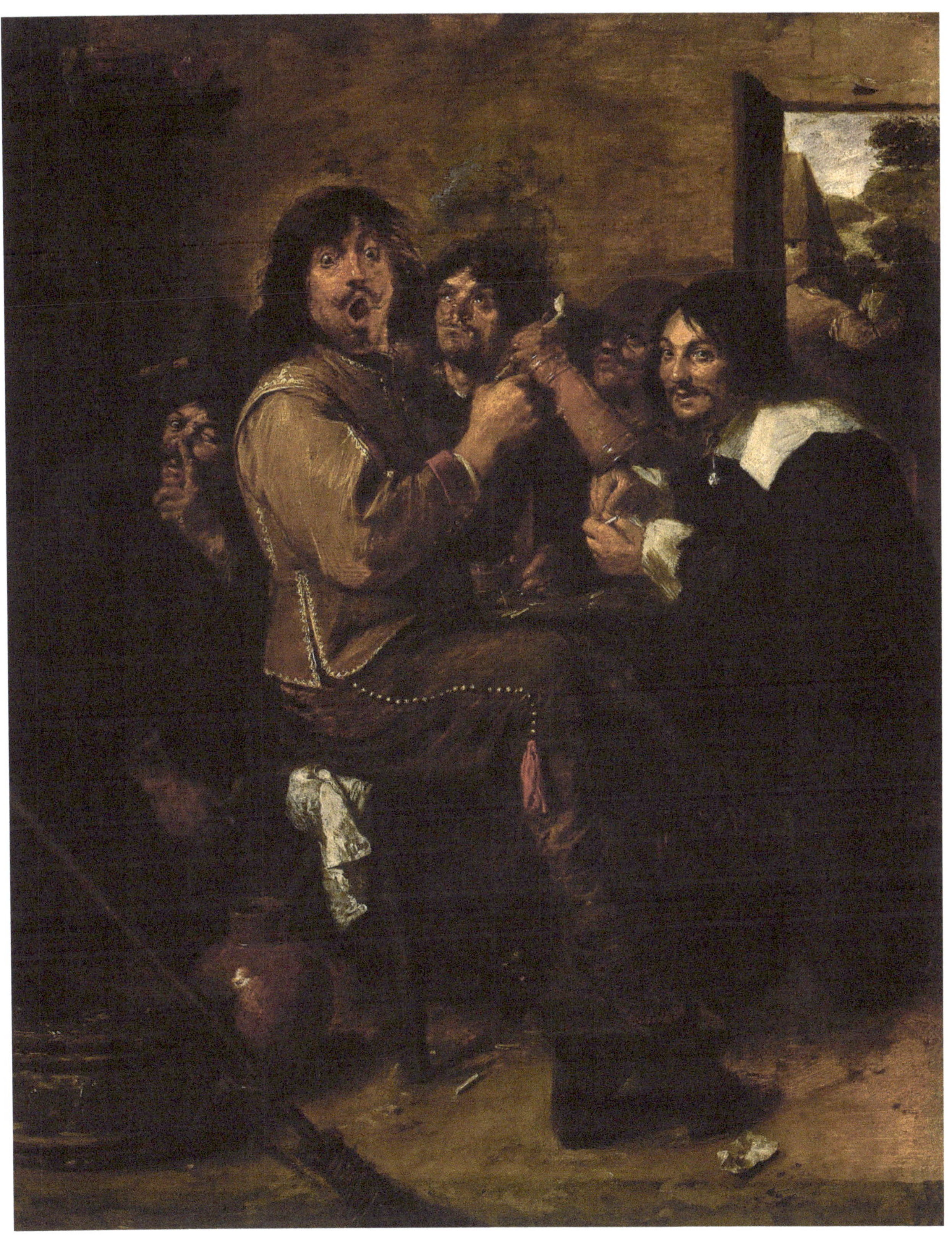

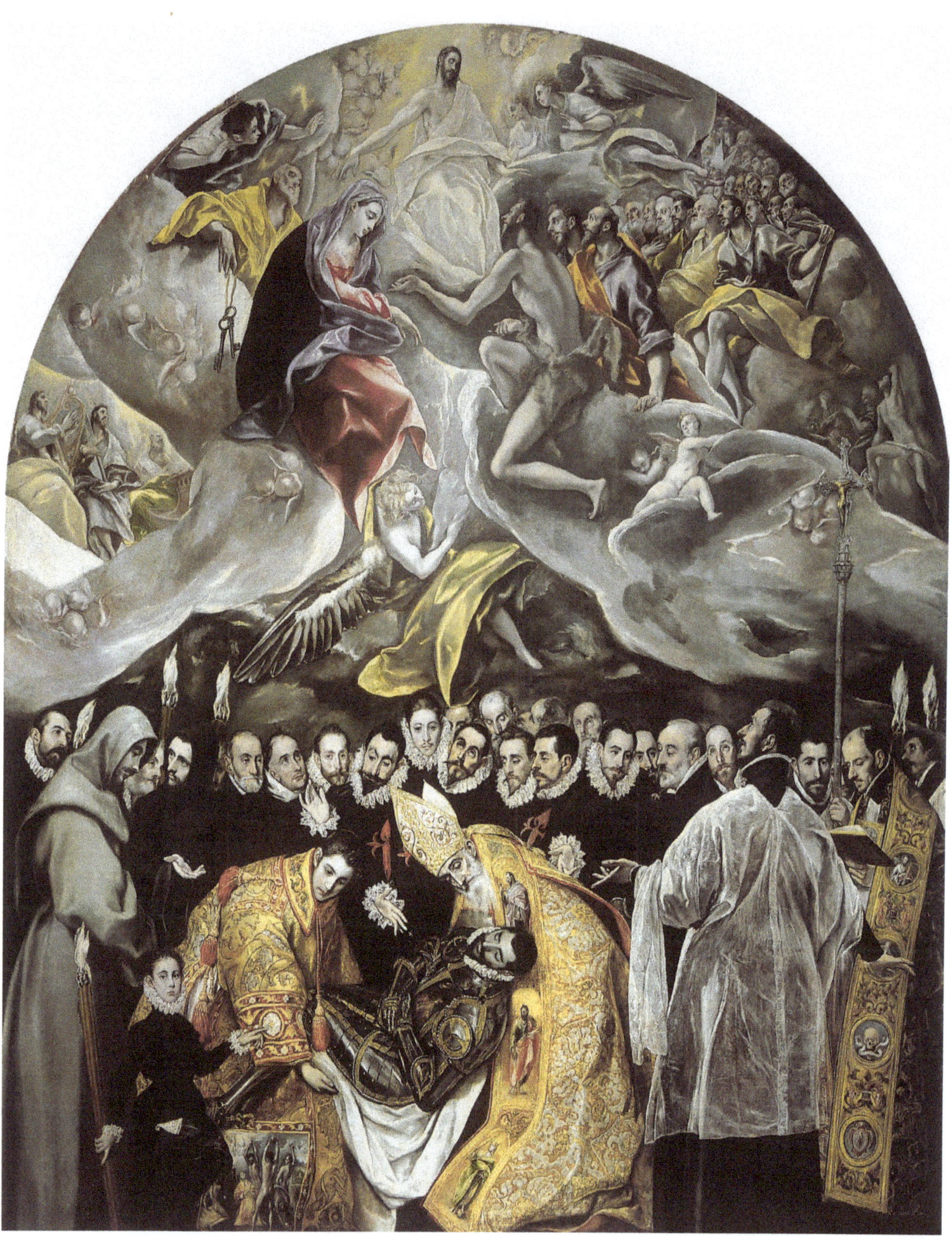

SPAIN

El Greco

(1541 Crete – 1614 Toledo)

El Greco was the name commonly given to Domenikos Theotokopoulos. He was born in Crete, between 1545 and 1550, and announces his Cretan origin by his signature in Greek letters on his most important pictures, especially on the St. Maurice. He appears to have studied art, first of all, in Venice, and on arriving in Rome in 1570 is described as having been a pupil of Titian.

The first picture commissioned from him by Philip II was the Parting of the Rock (1577), destined for the sacristy of the Cathedral of Toledo, which aroused the wonder of the Spaniards with its bright, golden colouring. His second commission, a depiction of the Martyrdom of St. Maurice and his Wife, was carried out by him in 1580-1581 in the Spanish style. It illustrates the darkened colour harmonies used by Spanish painters in order to breathe a sign of life into them in the manner of a wood carving.

El Greco's portrayal of the martyrdom was a complete failure with his royal patron but the Archbishop of Toledo showed him favour and commissioned him to paint the Burial of Count Orgaz (c. 1586). This painting is certainly one of his main works. The church pictures to be particularly noted are The Ascension of Maria (1607-1613), The Crowning of the Virgin, and The Holy Trinity (1577-1579), as well as the Crucifixion, the Pouring out of the Holy Ghost, the Resurrection (1584-1594), and finally the St. Francis.

It cannot be denied that all these works, despite their occasional spooky and ghostly characters, make a monumental impression. Extremely impressive is El Greco's skill with portraits, which can be clearly seen in the Portrait of an Elderly Nobleman (1585-1590). What made him appeal so much to the taste of his time are the passionate personalities and colouristic uniqueness that bring out shattering harmonies, with much use of brown-red, golden ochre, madder red, black and white hues.

◀ **El Greco,**
The Burial of Count Orgaz, 1586-1588.
Oil on canvas, 480 x 360 cm.
Iglesia de Santo Tomé, Toledo.

Diego Velasquez

(1599 Sevilla – 1660 Madrid)

Of Velázquez' two teachers, Pacheco and Herrera the Elder, one followed the Italian and the other the Spanish nationalistic direction. But only the latter had a decisive influence on the development of Velázquez. His artistic manner of expression was developed out of his naturalism. Velázquez was able to find the individual aspect of his subjects with such certainty that he was able to paint their pictures with broad brush strokes without afterwards having to change anything, working his colours in such a way that the result was a smooth surface.

Velázquez came to the attention of King Philip IV through the portraits he had painted in 1622, and he became Court Painter in the following year. Through his art and his personality Velázquez achieved such a position of trust that the King even appointed him House and Travel Marshal in charge of the pomp and organization of the Court. His main work in these years is the picture known as The Feast of Bacchus ("Los Borrachos"). His new style was already fixed by the time Velázquez undertook a journey to Italy, a year after completion of this picture. In Rome he then painted The Forge of Vulcan (1630), a well-known piece. This Forge of Vulcan is a work that is a close relative to The Drinkers in the delineation of the bony, broad-shouldered and understated figures. Despite such pictures, Velázquez was not lacking

a religious depiction in the deepest sense within his basic outlook, which is evident in the thrilling work, Christ on the Cross. Despite such interludes, his sense of reality usually gained the upper hand, aided by the necessity to paint portraits. One of the exceptions to this rule is the only depiction of an historical event of his times: the Surrender of Breda, which, if one observes the individual parts, consists of a collection of portraits. How important realism was to Velázquez is shown by the forest of upright lances in the background.

As a portrait painter at the Spanish Court, Velázquez had to battle with the complicated society that existed there. From a man like Philip IV one could extract just as little intellectual capital as from his sycophants, especially when the King or his devious First Minister, the Duke of Olivares, had to be painted on horseback. Still more difficult was Velázquez's position with the Queen, the princesses and the ladies of the Court, because this also involved the battle with the quite pompous apparel of the times, with shapeless petticoats and the deep sighs of inhibiting stays as seen in the Portrait of the Infanta Margarita as a Young Girl.

Perhaps it was in moments like this that he got the idea for the picture which became famous under the name Las Meninas and which showed a view

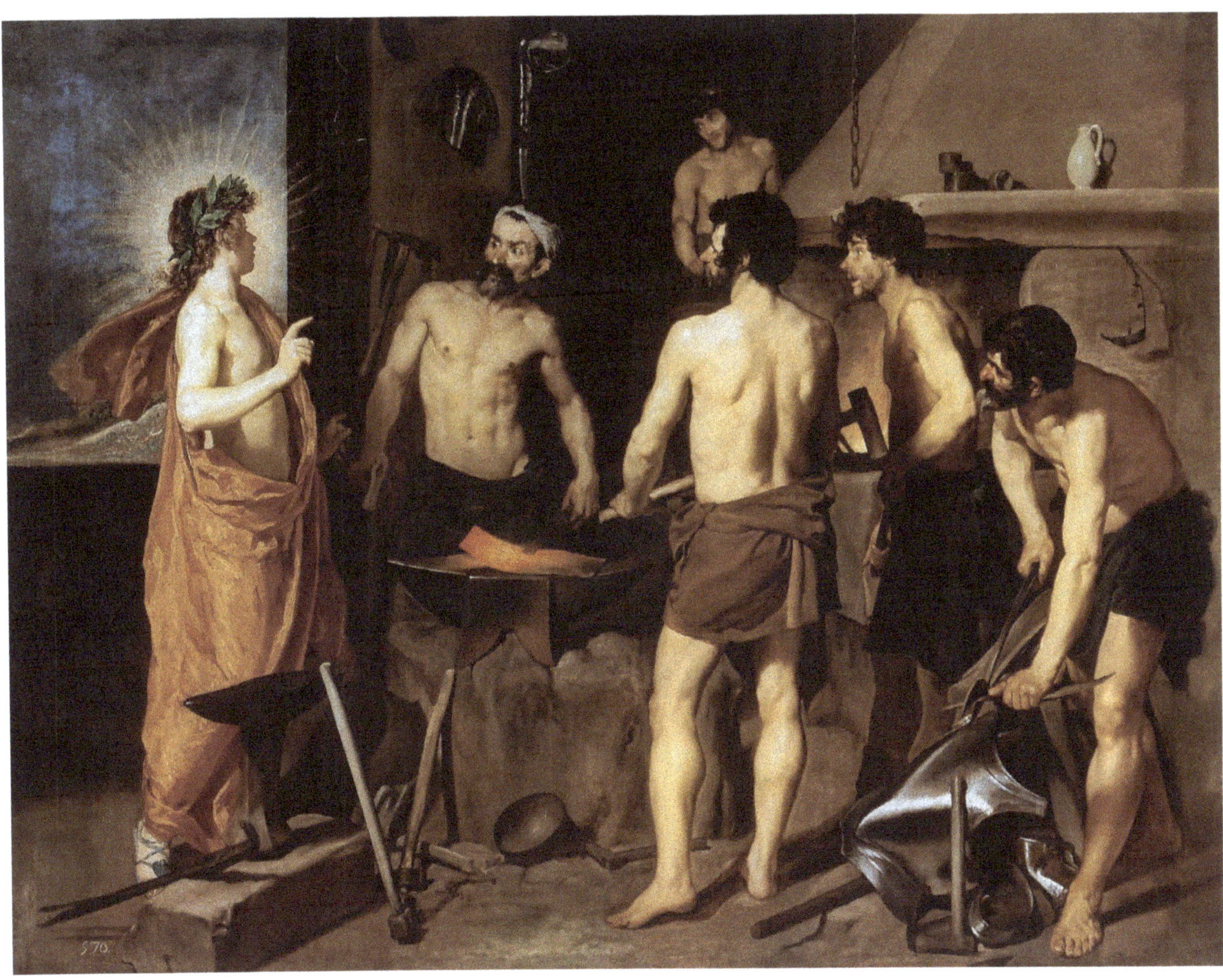

▲ **Diego Velázquez**, *The Forge of Vulcan*, 1630.
Oil on canvas, 223 x 290 cm. Museo Nacional del Prado, Madrid.

of his studio in the royal palace and the life at the Spanish Court. Las meninas are the two maids who were meant to keep the two small princesses amused while their royal parents were modelling for Velázquez standing at his easel. A mirror at the rear of the room shows the figures of the royal couple in unmistakable clarity. A dwarf with his foot on a dog and various courtiers in the middle and background complete the appearance of serious and grotesque figures.

In 1649 Velázquez undertook a second journey to Rome. There he was granted the opportunity to paint Pope Innocent X. In this portrait he created possibly the greatest masterwork of his career. Among the famous papal portraits it is perhaps the only one that can be compared with Raphael's Julius II and Leo X with two Cardinals.

A large celebration at the court exhausted him to such an extent that he died on August 6, 1660 of a fever.

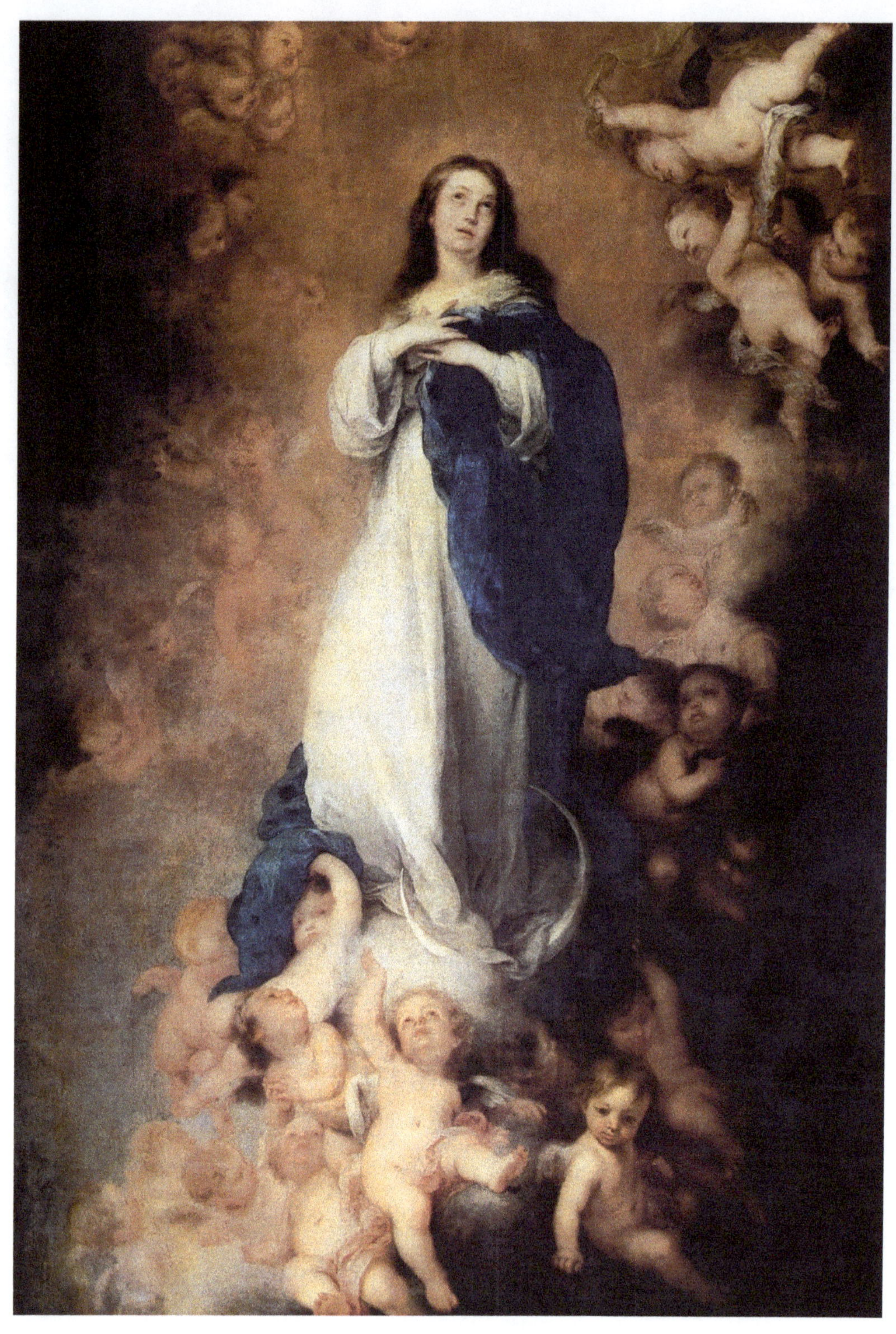

▲ **Bartolomé Esteban Murillo**, *The Immaculate Conception*, c. 1678.
Oil on canvas, 274 x 190 cm. Museo Nacional del Prado, Madrid.

Bartolome Esteban Perez Murillo

(1618 – 1682 Seville)

Murillo was doubtlessly the most versatile in his choice of materials as well as in his depiction of the life of the people, and for this reason his contemporaries and followers appreciated him more than Velázquez, who was limited by the life of the Court at the time.

Painter and draughtsman, Murillo began his art studies under Juan del Castillo, with some influence from Zurbarán. He painted in Seville, especially religious themes such as the Immaculate Conception, illustrating the doctrines of the Counter-Reformation. He was also one of the greatest portrait painters of his time.

Murillo's work is divided into three different styles: the cool (frio), the warm (calido) and the vaporous (vaporoso). The vaporous (or misty) style corresponds approximately to the best of Rembrandt's style called warm, transparent light-darkness.

Murillo's first success was a cycle of eleven pictures for the nave of the Franciscan Monastery, depicting events from the lives of famous followers of these monks and the affiliated orders of nuns. One of the masterworks of this series is the Death of St. Clara (1645).

The nationalism in Murillo's pictures is well expressed in his depictions such as Madonna with Child (c. 1670), in which he shows the Madonna as a woman of the people. With a humour that is seldom in evidence in Spanish painting, Murillo also imbued his images of dirt and rags, miserliness and gluttony with a poetic sheen. His masterwork in the presentation from the life of the Holy Family, an example of his "warm" style but already with a strong tendency towards coloured wispiness: this is the Birth of the Virgin (c. 1660) in which he shows a Spanish nursery.

Murillo achieved a balance in his artistic gifts around 1670. The following decade can rightly be called his most brilliant period in which one masterpiece directly followed another. Between 1670 and 1674, he created a large series of pictures for the Caridad Hospital in Seville. Two of these are wide pictures with a large number of figures and are evidence of Murillo's depiction of actual life, his power of composition and his ability to arrange a large crowd of people around a focal point. One of these two pictures, known in Spain as La Sed ("the thirst"), depicts the miracle of Moses drawing water from a stone in the desert.

Like Velázquez, Murillo died at the height of his fame. He fell from the painting platform during the creation of an altarpiece in the Capuchin Church in Cadiz. He did not recover from this fall and died on April 3, 1682.

Franscisco de Goya y Lucientes

(1746 Fuendetodos – 1828 Bordeaux)

Goya is perhaps the most approachable of painters. His art, like his life, is an open book. He concealed nothing from his contemporaries, and offered his art to them with the same frankness. The entrance to his world is not barricaded with technical difficulties. He proved that if a man has the capacity to live and multiply his experiences, to fight and work, he can produce great art without classical decorum and traditional respectability. He was born in 1746, in Fuendetodos, a small mountain village of a hundred inhabitants. As a child he worked
in the fields with his two brothers and his sister until his talent for drawing put an end to his misery. At fourteen, supported by a wealthy patron, he went to Saragossa to study with a court painter and later, when he was nineteen, on to Madrid.

Up to his thirty-seventh year, if we leave out of account the tapestry cartoons of unheralded decorative quality and five small pictures, Goya painted nothing of any significance, but once in control of his refractory powers, he produced masterpieces with the speed of Rubens. His court appointment was followed by a decade of incessant activity – years of painting and scandal, with intervals of bad health.

Goya's etchings demonstrate a draughtsmanship of the first rank. In paint, like Velázquez, he is more or less dependent on the model, but not in the detached fashion of the expert in still-life. If a woman was ugly, he made her a despicable horror; if she was alluring, he dramatised her charm. Like Velázquez, he concentrated on faces, but he drew his heads cunningly, and constructed them out of tones of transparent greys. Monstrous forms inhabit his black-and-white world: these are his most profoundly deliberated productions.

His fantastic figures, as he called them, fill us with a sense of ignoble joy, aggravate our devilish instincts and delight us with the uncharitable ecstasies of destruction. His genius attained its highest point in his etchings on the horrors of war. When placed beside the work of Goya, other pictures of war pale into sentimental studies of cruelty. He avoided the scattered action of the battlefield, and confined himself to isolated scenes of butchery. Nowhere else did he display such mastery of form and movement, such dramatic gestures and appalling effects of light and darkness. In all directions Goya renewed and innovated.

Francesco de Goya y Lucientes, ▶
1746-1828, Romanticism, Spanish, *El Aquelarre (The Witches' Sabbath)*, 1797-1798.
Oil on canvas, 44 x 31 cm.
Fundación Lázaro Galdiano, Madrid.

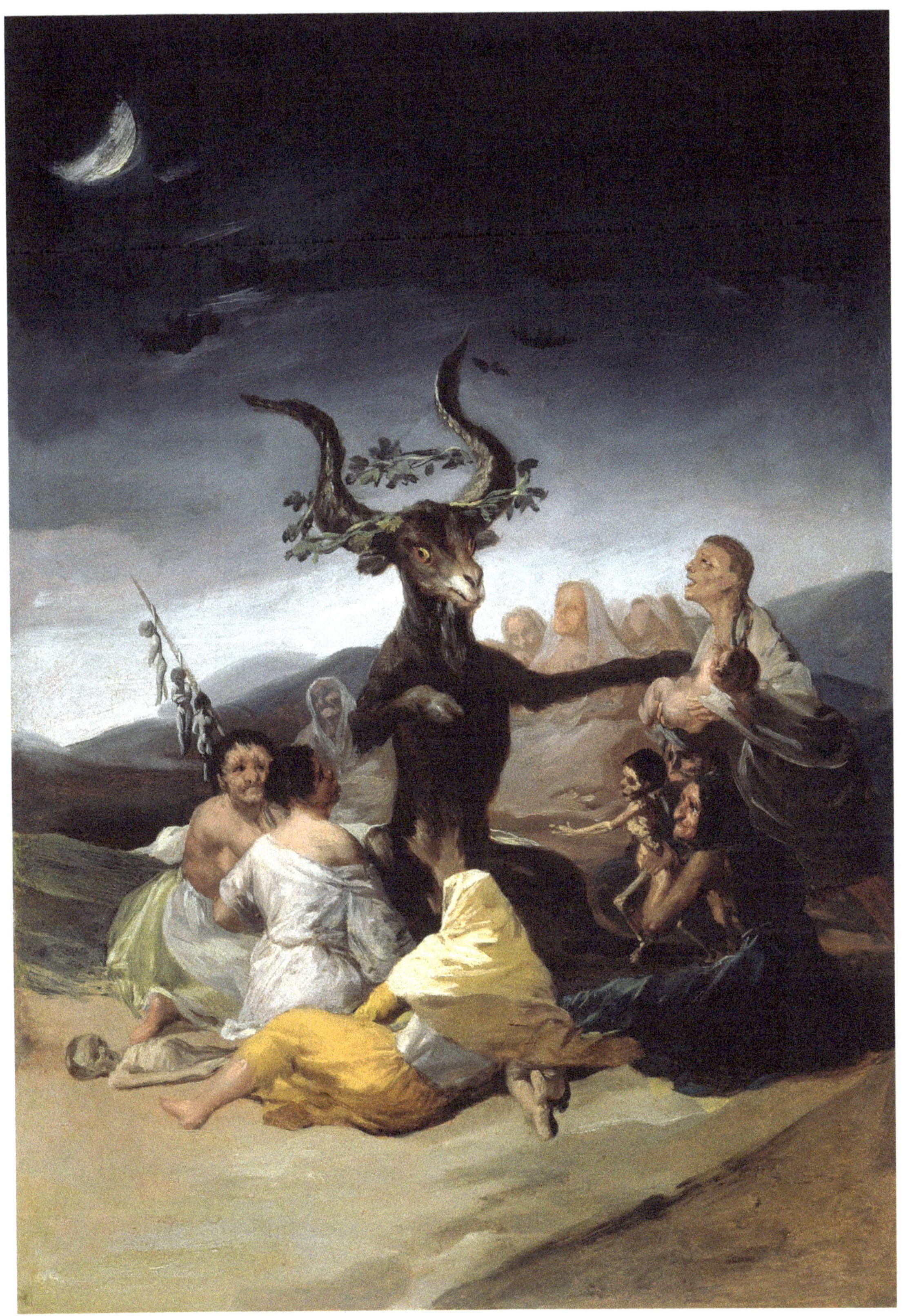

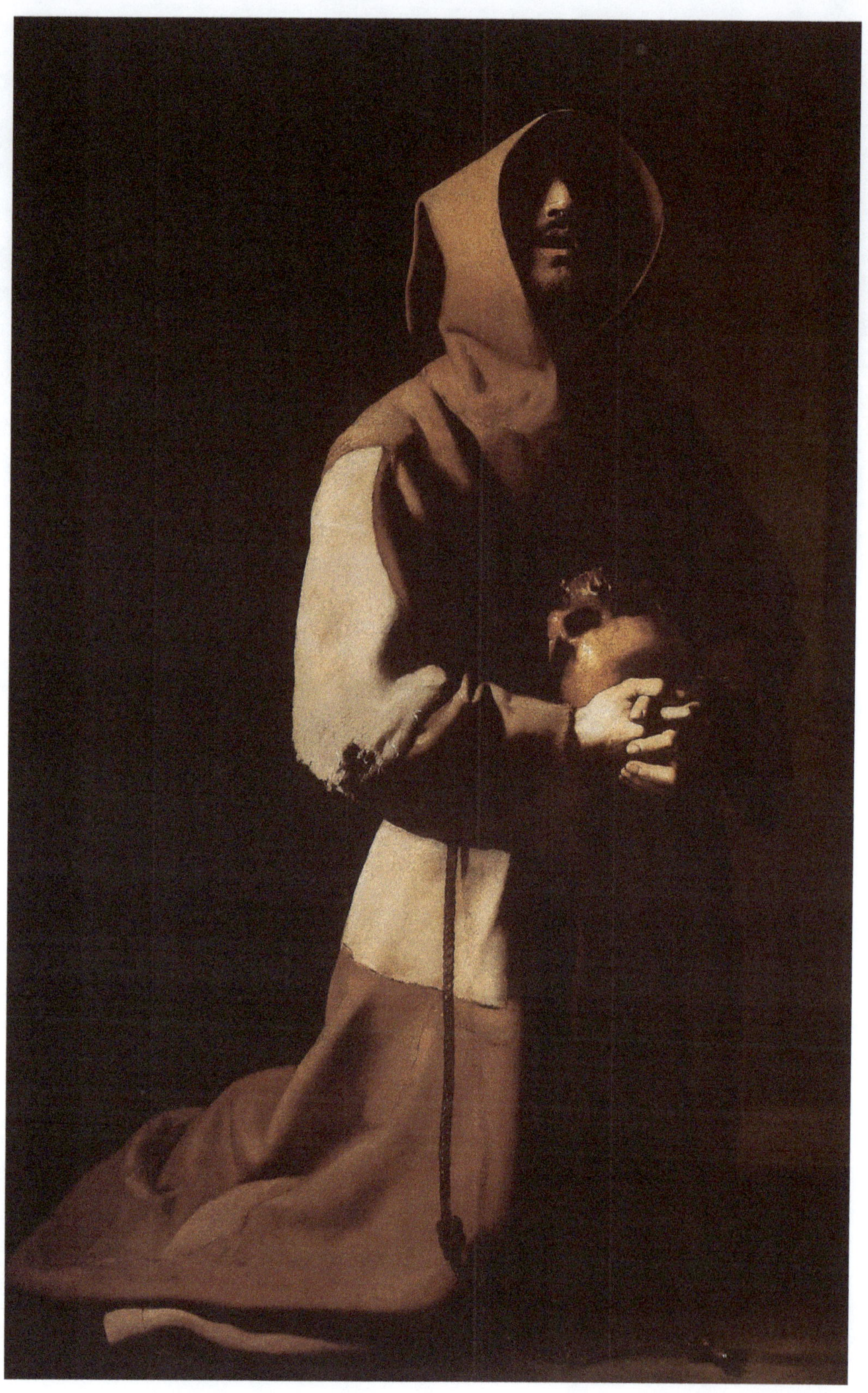

Francisco Zurbaran

(1598, Fuente de Cantos— 1664, Madrid)

I n Zurbaran's childhood he set about imitating objects with charcoal; that is why his father sent him, still young, to the school of Juan de Roélas in Seville. Francisco soon became the best pupil in the studio of Roélas, surpassing the master himself; and before leaving him he had achieved a solid reputation in Seville.

He may have had there the opportunity of copying some of the paintings of Caravaggio; at any rate he gained the name of "the Spanish Caravaggio", owing to the forcible realistic style in which he excelled. His subjects were mostly of a severe and ascetic kind – religious vigils, the flesh chastised into subjection to the spirit – the compositions seldom thronged, and often reduced to a single figure. The style is more reserved and chastened than Caravaggio's, the tone of colour often bluish to excess. Exceptional effects are attained by the precise finish of foregrounds, largely massed out in light and shade. Towards 1630 he was appointed painter to Philip IV; and there is a story on one occasion the sovereign laid his hand on the artist's shoulder, saying, "Painter to the king, king of painters."

It was only late in life that Zurbaran made a prolonged stay in Madrid. He died probably in 1662 in Madrid.

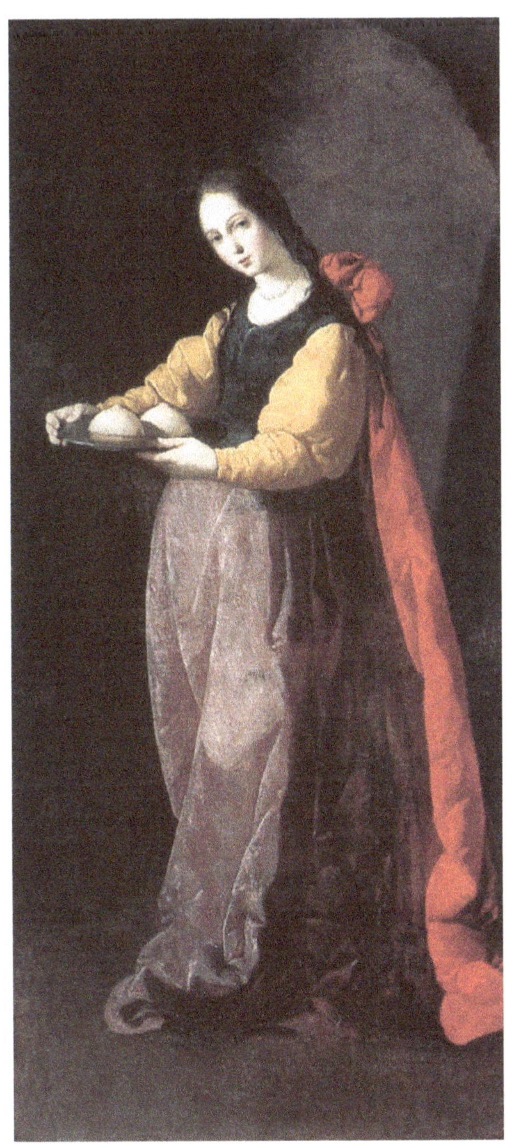

◄ **Francisco de Zurbarán**, 1598-1664,
Baroque, Spanish, St Agatha, c. 1634.
Oil on canvas, 129 x 61 cm.
Musée Fabre, Montpellier.

▲ **Francisco de Zurbarán**,
St. Francis in Meditation, c. 1635-1640.
Oil on canvas, 152 x 99 cm.
The National Gallery, London.

LIST OF ILLUSTRATIONS

ART HISTORY COLLECTION

Abstract Art

Art Deco

Art Nouveau

Baroque

Byzantine Art

Chinese Art

Cubism

Dada

Early Italian Art

Egypt Art

Expressionism

Gothic Art

Greek Art

Impressionism

Indian Art

Naive Art

Neoclassicism

Persian Art

Post-Impressionism

Realism

Renaissance

Pre-Raphaelites

Rococo

Roman Art

Romanesque Art

Romanticism

Surrealism

Symbolism

The Fauves

The Viennese Secession